Herzog &
de Meuron

Herzog &
de Meuron

Royal Academy of Arts

CONTENTS

PRESIDENT'S FOREWORD

For Herzog & de Meuron, an exhibition is a project in itself. As with all their new projects, site, time frame and brief provide an opportunity to reimagine architecture. We are therefore delighted to have collaborated with the practice to make the first major London survey of their work for almost twenty years.

Over this time, Herzog & de Meuron have grown into a global firm with more than 600 collaborators. Yet they remain rooted in Basel, home of their founders Jacques Herzog and Pierre de Meuron, who have built more than forty projects in the Swiss city and established an archive and research space there.

Herzog & de Meuron are renowned for staying one step ahead, challenging themselves and constantly questioning the purpose and meaning of architecture, which is why we were particularly keen to show their work at the Royal Academy, a place that never stands still or rests on its laurels. The exhibition and its catalogue represent a huge collective effort on the part of both Herzog & de Meuron and the Royal Academy. We thank Jacques Herzog, Pierre de Meuron and their partners for allowing us to exhibit works from their office and *Kabinett* archive, as well as their exhibitions and publications team led by Esther Zumsteg, Christine Binswanger, Donald Mak, Mathieu Bujnowskyj and Saakib Sait. The exhibition was initiated by our former Head of Architecture, Kate Goodwin, with Rhiannon Hope. Following the Covid-19 pandemic, it was reconceived with new dates and in different galleries, where it has been co-curated with Herzog & de Meuron by Vicky Richardson, Head of Architecture and Drue Heinz Curator, with Rose Thompson. The exhibition was managed by Rebecca Bailey with Guy Carr. Image rights and reproduction were managed by Giulia Ariete with graphic design by Daly & Lyon.

Herzog & de Meuron have experimented and tested the potential of augmented reality as part of the design process, and developed an app that visitors can download before entering the exhibition; we are grateful to them for their encouragement and enthusiasm for pushing the boundaries of exhibition-making. RA Publications have produced this handsome accompanying publication in collaboration with Herzog & de Meuron, with design by Perrin Studio. We thank Ricky Burdett, Ila Bêka and Louise Lemoine, Beate Söntgen, Marc Forster and Henrik Schødts for their illuminating texts on the practice and its innovative designs.

As ever, we are indebted to our sponsors for their generosity, and we extend our deepest gratitude to Stefan Bollinger, Laura and Scott Malkin and the Swiss Arts Council Pro Helvetia.

Rebecca Salter PRA
President, Royal Academy of Arts

ACKNOWLEDGEMENTS

In addition to those thanked in the President's Foreword on page 9, the Royal Academy is exceptionally grateful to the following individuals for their invaluable assistance in the making of this exhibition and its accompanying publication: Roman Aebi, Giorgio Azzariti, Erika Bolton, Stephanie Bush, Martin Cassani, Polly Chiapetta, Nancy Cooper, Phil Cooper, Simeon Corless, Wayne Daly, Florence Dassonville, Phil Drewry, Caroline Ellerby, Ashley Elliot, Fiona Elliott, Benji Fox, Dan Gunning, Max Holder, Ainsley Johnston, Sarah Kim, Roger Kneebone, Carola Krueger, Stefanie Manthey, Nikola Miloradovic, Sigrid Muller, Anna Nesbit, Martin Perrin, Jane Quinn, Lucy Record, Peter Sawbridge, Günter Schwob, John Shevlin, Andrea Tarsia, Milou Teeling, Victor Tessler, Rachel Walker, Edward Wang, and Michelle Young.

1

MAKING WINDOWS IN SANDCASTLES

Herzog & de Meuron's *Kabinett* is a repository of creativity. Part-archive, part-laboratory, part-studio, part-display, it documents more than 450 of over 600 projects designed since the office was founded in 1978. Occupying the lower floors of a robust concrete building conceived by the practice, at the heart of the emerging, creative Dreispitz district they masterplanned on the edge of the Swiss city of Basel that has become synonymous with them, the *Kabinett* redefines the paradigm of an architectural collection just as Herzog & de Meuron has redefined the paradigm of thinking and making architecture for the last decades.

> **Jacques Herzog**
> Founder
> The entire collection – photography, art, architecture – reflects our interest in the diversity of the world, in the social, but also in the normality of all of us. That's why we call it the *Kabinett*. It's a cabinet and not just an archive. We want to see these things in a certain context and we want to keep them together. That's why we built a new building rather than refurbish an old one. We wanted to make it a space, a physical space.

For the architects, the term 'cabinet' stands for something intimate, something that has emerged and been preserved with great care over the course of many decades and, above all, something that should remain 'fruitfully workable'. The plan is to document a large proportion of Herzog & de Meuron's past and future output, with drawings, models and artefacts slowly filling the building. The core (*fundus*) is made up of the office's architectural output, while the collection includes works by artists Rémy Zaugg, Andreas Gursky and Ai Weiwei as well as a rare archive of nineteenth- and twentieth-century photography offering a raw perspective of human life and the built environment before the age of the image. In time, the entire collection (a non-profit foundation established by the founding partners) will be made available to Basel's globally respected Kunstmuseum as part of its public art collection, ensuring the 'local' architectural practice occupies a place in the city's cultural life in perpetuity.

JH Rémy Zaugg was exceptional. He was like a third partner in the early days with Pierre and myself, before we had other partners. Ai Weiwei is a kind of Chinese version of Rémy because he is also a tough cookie, powerful intellectual, strong thinker and very conceptual. Sometimes I came home with a headache because Rémy was smoking in the car while Pierre was driving. We talked about everything related to the projects that we eventually did together. It was just about life. With Weiwei, we went to the most

2

2   Rémy Zaugg, *Vom Tod II* (*About Death II*) (1999, 2002, 2004), an installation of 27 paintings inside the *Kabinett*

3   Conceptual models exploring massing, envelope, functional distribution, circulation and façade for the Blavatnik Building, Tate Modern, London

remote areas in China: to Jinhua, to Jingdezhen, the porcelain city where the Ming dynasty produced amazing objects. We learned about Chinese culture and art. Too few Europeans know how innovative China has been. Weiwei opened our eyes. With others like Thomas Ruff and Andreas Gursky, our collaborations sometimes resulted in an urban design approach, perceptual concept or play on the senses, but not necessarily the integration of art or artwork in our architecture.

Arranged with the scientific precision of a mineralogist in rows of plywood vitrines, each of the *Kabinett*'s displays illustrates the narrative behind a design project. Neatly aligned wood, cardboard, plaster, metal and coloured-foam models show how the muscular weave of the 'Bird's Nest' National Stadium's external structure in Beijing (developed with Ai Weiwei for the 2008 Olympic Games) or Prada Aoyama's seductive glass skin in Tokyo (2003) were worked and reworked. The process of elimination and reduction is not explained as such, but the attentive eye can discern a pattern of critical thinking that underlies the design trajectory.

Elsewhere in the *Kabinett*, the typological alternatives of the 56 Leonard Street tower in New York City (2017) expose the process of sculptural refinement that shaped the identity of the 57-storey residential high-rise. Despite a new generation of 'super-tall-skinny' skyscrapers vying for attention in Manhattan, the offset stacking of individual apartments and protruding terraces create a pixelated visual effect that is far more distinctive and original than its aspirational competitors. Nearby, in the *Kabinett*, the radically diverse schemes for the Tate Modern Switch House in London – from early versions of extruded glass boxes to the final brick-clad spiral of the realised Blavatnik Building (2016) – reveal how the architects experimented with its material in response to the changing urban context. Like exhibits in a natural history museum, these artefacts will become the subject of study by practitioners

3

and scholars interested in contextualising and interpreting Herzog & de Meuron's work in the future. They are a collective memory bank for the office itself to better understand the design processes that have constructed its own architectural heritage.

Of the many projects displayed in the *Kabinett*, a vitrine with distorted metal tubes stands out. The Schaulager, Laurenz Foundation in Dreispitz is a building in which art is stored but still accessible for the public to view. Completed in 2003, its heavy outer walls give the impression that the building emerges from the ground, and at the same time control the strict environmental conditions required to conserve art at ideal levels of light, humidity and temperature. The architects experimented with twisted metal profiles to create windows in the heavy façade, which as Jacques Herzog puts it, 'creates the sort of fuzzy edge you get when you run your finger along a sandcastle'.[1] It is an exercise in perceptual and environmental control, emphasising the designers' fascination with gravity and materiality: one of the many instances where Herzog & de Meuron has both reframed the paradigm of the programme (an art storage *and* exhibition space) and experimented with the process of turning abstract concepts into tangible architecture.

Each display in the *Kabinett* has a distinctive pedagogic and visual value – informative and seductive – exposing the labour-intensive research that lies behind the innovative architectural forms, textures and spatial experiences of many Herzog & de Meuron buildings. The narrative and experience are enhanced with the use of virtual-reality and augmented-reality tools developed by the in-house team to animate the static displays and engage the viewer in a 3D journey through as-yet-unbuilt projects.

JH   Virtual reality today is fascinating if you forget the technology and you just try to use it in a way that involves you as a human. I think it's more interesting when you try to understand which senses are missing. In the design for the Autobahnkirche [motorway chapel], we used VR to test what people can touch; it helps us literally enter a new world. I compare it with a Harry Potter movie where students catch the Hogwarts Express by entering a new world through a brick wall at King's Cross Station. People are attracted by the magic, but even in the world of magic you remain a human and you depend on your senses; how they fall apart and how you reassemble them. It brings you back to these fundamental questions that have always been part of our experiments and research. Our architecture is very much oriented to all the senses.

4   Mock-up of the Blavatnik Building,
Tate Modern, testing the concrete
skeleton and perforated brickwok
of the inclined façade

4

It has become a trope to state that the practice's oeuvre eschews
stylistic definition. Yet, seeing over 500 projects together in one
space designed over an extended time-frame, a consistent design
research methodology emerges as a *fil rouge* that cuts across
projects of different sizes, uses and locations. Whether it's
London's Tate Modern Turbine Hall (2000) as a social condenser,
the gigantic urban billboard of the M+ museum of visual culture
in Hong Kong (2021), the relationship to light and materials for
patients in the REHAB Basel clinic (2002; extension 2020) and the
new children's hospital in Zurich (under construction), the sensual
pleasure and colours of the refurbished Stadtcasino in Basel
(2020) or the sensory dialogue of the as-yet-unrealised Calder
Gardens museum in Philadelphia, there is a relentless search to
experiment and innovate, to rethink the paradigm that makes
architecture real and socially responsive.

Herzog & de Meuron know 'how to make a concept physical',
as the *Guardian*'s normally acerbic architecture critic Rowan Moore
has observed:

> the best work is dazzlingly good, fertile in imagination, daring
> in its ideas, precise in conception and execution. They have
> a genius for making the materials and spaces of buildings
> perform the unexpected, which once done turns out to be apt
> for the lives their architecture serves. They are both intellectual
> and sensual; they know how to make a concept physical. Their
> understanding of human life is not, as it is for many architects,
> blandly optimistic. Their gamut of sensations includes the
> dark and the uncanny.[2]

This critical lens clarifies the intellectual backbone of an
international collective of nearly 600 designers and support staff,
run with great efficiency from its HQ in Basel. In 2022, the global
reach of the practice and the range of projects it undertakes was
made evident at a pin-up of over 90 projects currently on the

drawing board of all Herzog & de Meuron offices. They ranged from territorial and urban planning to offices, museums and household objects: from a city block infill development in Austin, Texas, to the National Library of Israel in Jerusalem; from a small church on a Swiss motorway to nose-to-tail tables and chairs that minimise material use and production waste. A section dedicated to competitions (won or lost) was a useful reminder that the practice has consistently procured a reasonable percentage of its work – about 25% – through a competitive process despite its reputation as one of the world's most established practices with blue-chip public and private clients.

Pierre de Meuron
Founder

I think architecture is one of the only professions that does competitions. I see competitions like fitness training. It's about competing with others, but it is mostly competing with yourself. It forces you to reflect and ask 'What is it?' It's just about you, the brief and the site. You have to be fit when you present. Sometimes we are good, sometimes we are less good. You have to have the conviction that this is the right solution. But also know how to present it, how to put it into plans, how to put it into a model, into images and virtual reality or whatever. How to present something which is still in your mind, which is not yet built. That's about being fit.

Unlike other high-profile design practices that have struggled with financial stability, Herzog & de Meuron has been historically as attentive to the balance sheet as to its research, innovation and experimentation. This strategy is not unique, but it has sustained the practice during a period of relatively exponential growth. Apart from the two founding partners, there are now five Senior Partners, ten Partners, and forty-eight Associates working on projects across Europe, the Americas and Asia. The executive team often poke fun at their inability to put a limit on what is the ideal maximum size for an architectural practice, and the goalposts keep changing. Recently the practice has announced that the founding partners – Jacques Herzog and Pierre de Meuron – are selling a proportion of their shares in the company to younger partners to ensure a gradual devolution from one generation to another, and that those individuals who have invested most in the design ethos of the company will lead the transition to its immediate and distant future.

PdM The economic dimension of the company is important. I believe it has to work economically, otherwise I cannot free myself to think and do things. It has to work like this from the beginning and I think we still do that. Whether you are an office of two or six hundred, I think there is the same mindset. There was never a set plan to grow. Who would have imagined that when Jacques and I met each other at the age of seven, we would do this? When we started the office in 1978, we just wanted to do the best we could and do the things we liked to do. I always used to say, around 20 years ago, that a hundred people would be the maximum. Then I said two hundred is the maximum. Who knows?

5

Growth itself is not a goal. I don't believe that you can only be
successful if you grow. We grow if we have a project and we
are lucky to still be able to make choices. We don't have to do it
if we think a project is not for us; if it doesn't fit with our way of
doing projects, we don't do it.

FROM LOCAL TO GLOBAL

Regularly listed amongst the most admired architects by their
peers across the globe, the practice continues to attract young
designers from an increasingly international pool, many seduced
by Basel's living and working conditions. The Herzog & de Meuron
workforce is very noticeable in the city, walking, cycling or even
swimming along the Rhine to its serene and domestic-scale
headquarters. The very nature of the internal office layout, with
relatively small, interconnected design studios and break-out
spaces, generates an unexpectedly informal atmosphere. Its spatial
dynamic mirrors the level of exchange and debate amongst the
large number of participants involved in making architecture at
Herzog & de Meuron. It's far more rough-and-ready than one would
anticipate from such an established Swiss 'brand' based in Basel.

In fact, though small, with a population of around 200,000,
Basel is anything but provincial. Home to two of the world's
pharmaceutical giants – Roche and Novartis – it straddles
Switzerland, France and Germany. Together with its sophisticated
artistic and musical heritage, it complements Zurich as the country's
banking and financial centre, and Geneva with the United Nations,

6

World Health Organization and other international institutions. Perhaps, as seven-year-old boys who played together after primary school, Jacques Herzog and Pierre de Meuron felt it in their bones, and despite its human scale, Basel ended up being the ideal place to nurture a global architectural practice.

PdM   Basel is a small city. Why stay here and why be active in this city? You have your roots. You are born here. In this rather small town, there is real excellence. There are strong institutions in arts, culture and music (world-class I would say). And then you have the life-sciences industry as well as interesting start-ups. So, this city is vibrant, is vital, is alive. Having these energies in your hometown is certainly one of the reasons why Jacques and I are still here and want to stay here. On the other hand, I'm happy to have had the opportunity to work with other ways of thinking, of seeing the world and its realities. It is necessary also not just to look back at yourself but to see yourself from a different point of view. That is so important.

From different social backgrounds, they have both observed and participated in the transformation of their city. Pierre de Meuron recently observed that he can look down on the neighbourhood in which he was raised from the top of one of the gigantic towers the practice has built for the Roche pharmaceutical complex.

De Meuron has always displayed an interest in the scientific method – concepts of geology, physics and thermodynamics litter his everyday conversation – while Jacques Herzog's artistic instinct

21

7

7   Models and full-scale mock-ups
    of the staircases for the
    Stadtcasino extension in Basel

8   Model of the Central Signal Box
    in Basel and photographs of
    Herzog & de Meuron buildings
    by Thomas Ruff displayed in the
    Kabinett

continues to drive his design approach (even though an obsessive interest in order reflects an early passion for biology). They studied architecture at ETH Zürich, and were inspired by the Italian architect and theorist Aldo Rossi – who promoted the concept of architecture as an urban artefact – and the German sociologist Lucius Burckhardt – who researched everyday man-made forms and structures. Armed with what Pierre de Meuron refers to as Rossi's 'hardware' and Burkhardt's 'software', the young designers developed a refreshingly broad spatial and social lens for their practice in the late 1970s at a time when the architectural profession was highly introverted and obsessed with formalism. The practice and its design leadership have of course evolved since then, but the commitment to research, testing and experimentation has survived. Their intellectual approach and natural interest in art and sciences has shaped their thinking and approach to architecture and provided the cultural framework for current and future generations of the practice.

JH   The good thing about art is that it is just what it is. It doesn't need to be explained. No one ever tells an artist what to paint, what to do. Literally, you must find your path. And that's exactly what I want to do. Indeed, I was always more attracted to art than to architecture. In the beginning I saw myself more as an artist than an architect. I showed my work in several exhibitions before I found out that I was not really an artist who could continue to develop his ideas in that field, but rather in architecture. I love painters. Very much. I soon discovered that I was not a painter, even if I did paint a lot at the beginning. I started to not like taking a brush and paint and applying it to a surface. This process was helpful to finally free myself from that obsession. I still try to find out what architecture is. In the past, architecture was more defined as a discipline. Our work is still based on this kind of uncertainty, looking for an experimental concept of what architecture could be.

9

From their earliest projects, Herzog & de Meuron have used Basel
as an urban laboratory with a series of distinctive yet understated
acupuncture projects. A successful design competition in 1979
(the third project for the young practice) re-envisaged the historic
Market Square, returning its hidden river to the public realm of the
city. They recently revisited the medieval core 40 years on with
a bold repositioning of the Stadtcasino, an equally subtle piece of
urban surgery that has transformed one of the city's public squares
and given a new lease of life to its nineteenth-century concert hall,
the much-loved Musiksaal. The project is a piece of internal and
external urban theatre where stitching is used to both recompose
the look and feel of the deep-red Belle Epoque seat covers and
wall linings – in the eleven-metre-high staircase lobbies – and
etched onto the timber façades inside and outside the building.

PdM   In the Stadtcasino, we contrasted a modern architectural
language (glass and steel) with a more mineral, traditional
architecture (solid walls with punched-in windows). For us, this
contemporary approach is not just about copying the old in a
nostalgic way, but an attempt to understand that there are
different kinds of architectures that respond to the local context,
like the very specific conditions of the Stadtcasino and its
settings. And I think you can also apply this approach to urban
and spatial planning in general.

9   Sammlung Goetz, Munich, a
    museum for a private collection
    of contemporary art

10 Turbine Hall, Tate Modern, London

10

In the 1980s and 1990s, the young practice completed several modest yet confident infill buildings which began to capture international critical acclaim.[3] The slim insertion of the timber-clad Apartment Building along a Party Wall in Basel is still as crisp, warm and filled with natural light today as it was when constructed in 1988. The moveable ironwork shutters of another, six-storey building deftly shoehorned into a tight urban gap in 1993 give identity and rhythm to an otherwise mundane Basel street. Together with the intriguingly sinuous copper-clad Central Signal Box (Basel, 1994) for Swiss Railways, the tectonically inventive Ricola Storage Building (Laufen, 1987) and Ricola-Europe SA (Mulhouse-Brunstatt, France, 1993) for herbal sweets, and the geometrically pure, light-filled Sammlung Goetz art gallery in Munich (1992), these projects created a fertile platform for the practice's entry on to a more global stage. It was with this portfolio that in 1994 the small, niche architectural practice was shortlisted for and then won the international competition for the conversion of the Bankside power station in London into Tate Modern: a project that transformed Herzog & de Meuron and transformed London.

More than any of the other competing entries by the some of the world's most respected architects – including OMA/ Rem Koolhaas, Renzo Piano, David Chipperfield and Tadao Ando – the Herzog & de Meuron scheme captured the essence of the Tate Modern brief set by its director Nicholas Serota: a profoundly urban building that responded to artists' need for space and light, a flexible and robust container that would transform the relationship between contemporary art and its diverse publics in London. Planned for two million visitors a year and now visited by nearly six million annually on a regular basis, the architects saw the potential of turning the cavernous Turbine Hall into what has become London's grandest public urban room and a permanent venue for new artist commissions. The delicate light beam at roof level was the only visible sign that the canonical power station had been converted. The twisting brick ziggurat of the Blavatnik Building,

25

11 The Education Tower at the
de Young Museum, San Francisco,
offers views over Golden Gate
Park, the city and the Bay

12 The existing brick façade and
metal roof extension of the
CaixaForum Madrid seem to lift
off the ground, drawing in visitors
from the Paseo del Prado

with matching heft and materiality of the original, now completes
the urban set-piece, opening up the entire complex to its
surroundings in South London and the River Thames. The opening
of Tate Modern in 2000 was a turning point for the practice, leading
to a different scale, scope and geographic reach of commissions
in a relatively short period of time.

Christine Binswanger
Senior Partner

When we were invited to submit a proposal for the Tate
competition, we hadn't designed a major art institution. We
said 'OK, of course'. And then, we won. The shock was how
the English press reported it: 'Who are these guys?' So many
things happened for the first time in our lives. You never forget
them. 'OK this is London, this is a major institution. Let's go.'
We've always been driven to get to a different place from where
we were. Should we try Asia? Hospitals? We always went for
opportunities, rather than follow a strategy.

The office's cultural buildings portfolio blossomed with the de Young
Museum in San Francisco (2005) followed by CaixaForum Madrid
(2008), the Pérez Art Museum Miami (2013) and the Park Avenue
Armory in New York City (2011–). The Tai Kwun – Centre for Heritage
and Arts (2018) and M+ in Hong Kong, the Museum der Moderne in
Berlin (2016–), the Vancouver Art Gallery (2014–), and the Calder
Gardens in Philadelphia extend and enrich the office's engagement
with the visual arts and the public realm. The Elbphilharmonie in
Hamburg (2016), Stadtcasino in Basel and National Library of Israel
in Jerusalem are major civic monuments that place culture at the
heart of their urban environments.

Despite the shared cultural and civic programmes of many
of these projects, it is difficult to discern a common architectural
language or a single artistic hand. As the sites become more
constrained by context or regulation, the designs seek tectonic
innovation and experiential intensification. They adhere more to a

philosophy than a style. As the projects get larger, they explore
a heightened sense of urbanity, complexity, porosity and density.
Each one of these buildings can be read as a piece of city that
connects and integrates users and consumers with diverse
interests and priorities. They invite random encounter, urban
surprise and unexpected liaisons.

    Sitting above a motorway tunnel running beneath Victoria
Harbour in Hong Kong, the M+ museum of visual culture turns
a Piranesian structural void – a 'found space' – into its main spatial
ordering device. It works like a square in a medieval city, attracting
and orienting visitors across its volumes and spaces with its
many entrances and exits. The façade of the main vertical building
is imaginatively transformed with LEDs and ceramic finishes into
Hong Kong's most visible electronic billboard, bringing art to the
city at the flick of a switch. Though based in Jerusalem, the
National Library of Israel reveals a similar response to context and
constraints. Located on the prime site next to Israel's Parliament
(Knesset), the plan and section evoke the multilayered complexities
of Old Jerusalem. Facing extreme local climate conditions and
conservative design constraints, the architects experimented with
a new type of carved stone façade that endows this civic institution
with gravitas and authority. The ground limestone and cement
skin provide shade and thermal mass to the main public reading
room with books stored in glass vitrines at lower level, maximising
visibility of the collection from above.

13

13   The entire LED-clad façade of
     the M+ museum for visual culture
     acts as a display for artworks that
     are integrated into Hong Kong's
     distinctive skyline

14   1111 Lincoln Road in Miami Beach,
     Florida, is a fully open concrete
     structure accommodating a car
     park and community activities

A similar investment in technical and spatial innovation runs through a series of earlier venues for mass public sports events. The colour-mutating Allianz Arena football stadium in Munich (2005) and the delicate Nouveau Stade de Bordeaux in France (2015) preceded the 'Bird's Nest' National Stadium in Beijing – possibly the most photographed of the practice's buildings. The list of public and private projects has continued to grow with unexpected, even provocative typological responses to at times conventional programmes resulting in idiosyncratic inventions like 1111 Lincoln Road in Miami Beach (2010) – a successful multistorey car-park-cum-shopping destination that eschews any commercial classification yet animates the city's urbane lifestyle.

ChB   1111 Lincoln Road in Miami Beach, the car-park project, was five years of passion, finding out how much you can stretch public life. Jason Frantzen had just joined the practice after having studied with Jacques and Pierre. After just a few days we already had the idea of 'overheight' that would turn the building into more than a car park – because you could use it for other community activities. Our client Robert Wennett called me when it was finished and said: 'People don't know what it is ... some have heard that it's a parking garage, but they think it's not finished.' So then I told him, you know what, why don't you put up a banner? 'Parking now open!' It's a vivid and happy memory of a dramatic moment.

Over the last twenty years, the number of urban studies and masterplans has expanded exponentially – in cities across Europe, Asia, the Americas and the Middle East. At the same time, the practice has deepened its own understanding of Switzerland with territorial studies, large-scale interventions in peripheries and a new generation of buildings that redefine some of the country's major cities. Their strategic approach is grounded in the research undertaken by ETH Studio Basel in 2006 and published in *Switzerland: An Urban Portrait*.[4] Through original mapping of

14

human settlements across the country, the study revealed – for the first time – that Switzerland is a continuous, relatively dense yet fragmented urban terrain, only partially defined by its alpine contours. Exploring the country's urban potential through five typologies – metropolitan regions, urban networks, quiet zones, alpine fallow lands, and resorts – the study has led to a new urban topography that challenges Switzerland's traditional model of social solidarity.

PdM   The city needs the rural and the rural needs the city. They need and complement each other. Our work on the Urban Portrait observed and mapped what is happening on the ground across the country. There are distinct geological typologies.

This analytical lens underpins many of Herzog & de Meuron's Swiss projects. The process of densification and transformation drives the new 'Plan Guide' for the historic city of Sion, deeply rooted in the territory of Valais, as does the bold intervention on Basel's skyline for Roche's new research and development complex. A cluster of tapering, white high-rise skyscrapers – significantly taller than the suburban surroundings – reorientate the urban geography of the city and represent a major commitment to Basel's economic and environmental well-being, reflecting the practice's commitment to sustainability that can be traced back to its earliest years.

15

PdM I think we have always been interested in sustainability, even without talking about it. In one of our earliest projects for Tavole – the Stone House we completed in 1988 – we took a very pragmatic and straightforward approach in using a dry-stone wall construction. It certainly had an aesthetic quality, but we were inspired by the unfinished buildings with concrete frames that you see in the region. We took a very 'economic' approach to the existing *rifugio*, which was a ruin. Economy shares the same prefix as ecology (eco = 'house' in Ancient Greek). It would have been too costly to bring new materials up to the site. It would have created traffic with trucks going up and down the mountain. So, we reused what was already there. Making the best out of what is there defines sustainable thinking at Herzog & de Meuron.

Today we go beyond this. In projects like the Hortus [House of Research, Technology, Utopia and Sustainability] timber office building in Allschwil, we experiment with using as little steel as possible, with finding new kinds of cement which work at lower temperatures. We collaborate with people who make earth bricks, who are involved in production and not too much theory. There is a lot to do, to test and to invest. We are not fully there yet, but it's a start. We have to put pressure on the market and on our clients.

CONNECTING THE SOCIAL TO THE PHYSICAL

More than any other building typology, the hospital connects the social and the physical in visceral ways. With REHAB Basel, designed in 1998, Herzog & de Meuron began a process of investigation into how architecture can contribute to patients' well-being and recovery, humanising the experience for doctors, nurses and family members and rethinking the spatial requirements of healthcare provision. It is a holistic process that involves re-evaluation of the spatial, tactile and visual dimensions of care and recovery.

The Basel clinic accommodates patients who have experienced life-changing accidents and need to learn how to become independent. Many are wheelchair-users, others need to lie on their back for long periods to recover. The delicate, two-storey timber structure was designed as an 'open, permeable and breathing' building where patients and their families can be alone or in company. Views to the sky and over the landscaped courtyard through windows, ceilings and open terraces maximise access to daylight and nature, while the predominant use of timber contributes to a more domestic feel than an institutional atmosphere. Completed over twenty years ago, some of its medical staff still work in the building and testify to the beneficial impact on generations of users.

PdM   It was the Clinical Director who made us understand what it's like when your spine is severed and you are paralysed. You start a completely new life. We had to understand this perception. I remember when I visited the old rehab centre, a young man there had just had a motorcycle accident. He had to lie on his back for weeks without being able to turn his head. So, the question was, 'What is the ceiling?' You know, for him, the ceiling is the only things he sees.

ChB   I think the greatest satisfaction you can have as an architect is when people who use your building on a daily basis still love to use it after years or even decades. This is the case with REHAB – which turned 20 last year!

JH   [At REHAB] we came up with a new hospital typology, largely defined by flat volumes. Like landscapes with numerous courtyards. Each of them different in design, material, detailing, vegetation, lighting. A building with spaces so different and distinct creates an intensity and diversity of perception for patients who have been forced to surrender the mobility they once took for granted. There is practically no other building by Herzog & de Meuron that embodies such a holistic combination of landscape, city and interior. And which provides an experience equally accessible to all those who live and work in those spaces. Patients, doctors, healthcare workers, visitors.[5]

Many of these architectural themes have been further developed and integrated at scale in a new series of commissions in Europe and the US. In the Kinderspital Zürich and the New North Zealand Hospital in Hillerød in Denmark (see pp 70–77), both due for completion in 2024, Herzog & de Meuron have set out to design hospitals that don't look or feel like hospitals. Set in the open countryside, Hillerød is a large and complex medical facility that will be visited by up to 10,000 people a day. Its progressive Danish

17

16 Pages 32–33:
    REHAB Basel, a clinic for
    neurorehabilitation and
    paraplegiology, was Herzog &
    de Meuron's first hospital project

17 The two-level horizontal
    structure allows wheelchair
    users, patients and staff to
    move easily across the building

18 A transparent ceiling skylight
    in the bedrooms offers views
    of the sky for patients lying in a
    horizontal position

19 Courtyards connecting indoor
    and outdoor spaces orientate
    visitors and allow daylight to
    penetrate the interior

clients were keen to promote a more integrated and open approach to healthcare, eliminating disciplinary borders and placing patients at the heart of the experience. Similar concerns drive the current expansion of the University Hospital in Basel and the UCSF Helen Diller Medical Center in San Francisco.

The apparent conflicts and synergies between institutional efficiency and humane environments become more pronounced in medical spaces for young people and children. Architecture here plays an even greater existential role. The Kinderspital will be the largest children's hospital in Switzerland. It has been carefully planned to break down the institutional scale whilst responding to the strict logistical requirements of a modern hospital complex – with an accident and emergency department, intensive care, operating theatres, canteens and facilities for parents and families of sick children. Yet the design team has invested most of its imagination and attention in the character, proportions and textures of individual patient rooms. Conceived like small houses with their own roofs and sloping internal ceilings, they are arranged on the top floor with generous part-opening windows giving a domestic rhythm to what is otherwise a sizeable 200-metre urban block. Internally, the materiality and positioning of seating, benches, lighting and window openings has been carefully calibrated to the experience of a child lying in bed. What can I see if I sit on the window bench? Can my family sit next to me and feel at home? Will this hospital make me feel better?

Despite the constraints imposed by hygiene and infection prevention, timber surfaces and natural materials are used throughout. The building communicates a human or even child-size sense of scale along its outer edges where the timber cladding, glass and concrete frame engage with the surroundings – the opposite experience of the conventional medical institution concealed behind unfriendly hospital walls.

ChB   The Kinderspital has the feel of a medieval city. All of a sudden a corridor widens, and a kind of square opens up to a small backyard type of space with a tree. Access to most of the more

18

19

than fifty hospital departments is via squares like this. In a non-institutional way, the spatial configuration and outdoor views help visitors to orient themselves. The specificity of these spaces emerges as a result of the many functional units, the adjacencies required and the flows between them.

JH The interesting thing about healthcare is that it's really about care. At this moment in history, I think it's important to focus on what architecture can do to be relevant. This is the main focus of the exhibition at the Royal Academy. Architecture is full of surprises. It is made up of details on every corner and at every angle. [In a child's hospital bedroom] it affects people in a very tangible way and shapes the experience of how they – doctors, children and parents – come together.

Over the years, Herzog & de Meuron has consistently invested in documenting the narrative and rationale behind its projects. Its partners invite critical discourse. Aside from a significant range of publications, films, articles, and a comprehensive website, the practice has used exhibitions as a form of investigation and experimentation. In one of the earliest exhibitions, 'Architektur Denkform' (Way of Thinking) at the Architekturmuseum in Basel in 1988, the architects silkscreened images of their projects onto the museum windows, engaging directly with the city at an urban scale. A display at Tate Modern in 2005 explored the creative process of making architecture by revealing the by-products or 'waste' produced during the course of their work. Their contribution to the Venice Architecture Biennale in 2012 told the story of the Elbphilharmonie project through uncensored press reports that demonstrated how it was the focus of public debate for years.

The exhibition at the Royal Academy started as an exploration of the sensory dimensions of architecture. One of the rooms includes the vitrines of the *Kabinett* with highlights of current, recent and historic projects. Another space contains a detailed exploration of the Kinderspital in Zurich, with full-scale mock-ups from parts of the patient rooms revealing how the architects have crafted a total environment for sensitive and humane care.

JH Architecture has such immense potential precisely because its sensual, material and spatial diversity is so similar to us human beings, so fragile and vulnerable. We can hear it, it can amplify and dampen sounds. It can store smells in stairwells and living rooms. Architecture has a smell; every room, every apartment smells different. Like the people who live there.

ChB I think we are still permanently trying to question ourselves. We do this amongst the Partners, but also with our younger colleagues. We enjoy it when they are present, alert and engaged. When people ask me: 'Why are you still here?', I reflect that I'm amongst the greatest people I could be with – their critical eyes, their brains are a great motivation for me and one of the factors behind our success. I love the complexity of interactions. I just love it. We are fairly well organised, but we don't follow any template that we then apply to projects nor to the other fields of action that make up a firm of our size. I would agree that we have become more strategic. We are a lot of people, we are in a different place now as a company, with different responsibilities.

By laying out the complexities of the programme of a modern hospital and inviting the visitor to understand the process of design, Herzog & de Meuron are once again using an exhibition to research and experiment with what it means to think and make architecture in the twenty-first century. There is a genuine and even naive desire that with more than 40 years of successful practice, the exhibition can say something new and refreshing about how meaningful architecture can be in making society fairer and our world more sustainable.

   With over 600 projects to show for it, Herzog & de Meuron can be confident that their buildings have contributed to our collective well-being, pushing the boundaries of what architecture can do to improve our experience of living and being in the world.

20 Herzog & de Meuron's campus at Rheinschanze 6 in Basel comprises both adapted and new buildings

21 View of workspaces in one of the buildings of the Herzog & de Meuron campus

20

22

ILA BÊKA AND
LOUISE LEMOINE

EMOTION OF SPACE

A Conversation with Jacques Herzog

Louise   Bonjour Jacques.

Jacques   Bonjour Louise, bonjour Ila. I like your topic of the 'Emotion of Space'. It is traditionally more associated with art than with architecture, or at least that is what I thought back in those days when I was still considering whether to go into art or architecture. But I was wrong. The more time I have spent exploring the potential of architecture, the more projects I have worked on, I came to understand how powerful an effect architectural space has on the human psyche.

You asked about emotional memory, whether I could remember some strong emotion I felt in relation to space. Of course, I have many and can perhaps describe them as unsettling (in German there is a good word for it – *unheimlich)* and nostalgic. These are the emotions that predominate in my memory of spaces. Nostalgic in the sense that it reminds me of something that is not there anymore. The passing of time somehow undermines the potentially positive emotions that a space might trigger, the feeling of: 'I have been in such a space before.' It makes me think about the huge amount of time that has elapsed. It's not necessarily a negative feeling but my emotions are cloudy, as if there were a filter in front of them.

I have the same feeling when I look at photographs, a kind of sadness. My brother loves photography; he collects photographs obsessively and eventually put together one of the world's largest collections of historical photography. He is as fascinated by it as I am depressed. The accumulation of a past that is dead and gone. I don't keep many photographs, except postcards, which I like

23

24

when they contain some information, such as a mountain pass or interesting details in architecture. But even those postcards, which are strongly anchored in my memory, are like heralds of death to me. Collecting, in the sense of accumulating objects from the past, is somehow alien to me. I'm not a collector; I'm more of a 'hunter' – always after something yet to be found. Even so, my understanding of space is deeply rooted in an awareness of memory and all the emotions that go with it. Regarding your initial question about architecture's capacity to provoke emotions, I don't think emotions are prompted by a specific form of architecture. It can be beautiful, ugly, banal, anything. That is also why our architecture has no signature style; I am not interested in style or references.

Ila   To go into more detail on this point, could you describe how you experience a space, physically, emotionally, when you discover it for the first time?

Jacques   Often, almost instantly, I get a sense of whether it feels good or bad, of whether I like it or not. Not aesthetically, but purely from my emotional perception of the space. In this context, architecture plays a key role. What influences how I feel the first time I enter a space? All the architectural elements come into play.

First the light, whether it is artificial or natural, and all the shadows it creates, the smell of the space that might overwhelm or bother me, the sound of a floor or of a wall – because you can also hear architecture. Then, the colours, the materials – people love

24 The final room of the Autobahnkirche, leading to the landscape outside

25 Still from Michelangelo Antonioni's *Identificazione di una donna* (*Identification of a Woman*), 1982

25

touching materials, feeling their texture. The forms, the shapes, the proportions and the furnishings inside also play a role. These latter are especially important with respect to psychological patterns. I often rearrange things around me. My wife must think: 'Why the hell is he doing that again?' When we go to a restaurant or arrive in a hotel room, for instance, I often feel tempted to change the position of the bed, or to rearrange tables and chairs, because they don't feel right in the space. Is my back in the right position with respect to the corner or to where the light comes in? Even when I am at a friend's house, in my mind I start to rearrange the position of the furniture – and it feels embarrassing to have such narrow-minded thoughts.

Another obsession of mine is to watch and analyse the movement of people in a space. Their performance, so to speak. In the city or out in the countryside, the way someone moves in the space reveals a lot about their psychology, about how they feel. What is their body language? Do they seek protection or enjoy exposure? Where do they choose to sit down? Protected by the crown of a tree or under a rock? Or rather on the grass, exposed to sunlight? It is like a kind of theatre, a play made of human gestures performed in the space. In architectural space, broadly speaking. These gestures are informed by architecture but in a reverse order they are transforming and shaping that very architectural space. That is why I often look at cities as petrified sculptures of psychological patterns and human behaviour.

Louise In your architectural practice, how do you manage to provoke emotions and awaken sensorial perception in the spaces you design?

Jacques I would say that filmmakers and painters can do this very well because they have a narrative that drives what they are doing. So, I understand why this is a central question for you, Ila and Louise, being filmmakers. Architectural interiors often play a key role in films. Think of Hitchcock and Powell and Pressburger,

41

26   27

who were a big inspiration for me in the 1980s, as well as Antonioni and Louis Malle. We all know the repertoire of their cabinets of horror. Interiors, especially with Hitchcock, with dark satin and velvet curtains, foyers with heavy neo-baroque wooden railings often curved and winding, foreshadowing worse things to come. Hitchcock loved this, but stairs also figure prominently in Antonioni's *Identificazione di una donna*. I was fascinated and inspired by cinema in my early years as an architect and even before when experimenting with video myself. One of our very early projects, the *Lego House*, is key to our understanding of architecture and in particular to how psychology and memory are related to architecture. Our *Lego House* features stills of a video filmed inside an architectural model built out of the Lego bricks that Pierre and I actually used as kids. The project is a testimony to that period and may embody just exactly what you are looking for in this conversation. We continue to apply this understanding of psychology in our work. For example, Miu Miu in Tokyo with its half-open cover, or the Prada Aoyama building, which is a more sci-fi-inspired psychological space. A more recent example is the use of mirrors in the Basel Stadtcasino. Mirrors also play an important role in my personal surroundings, not to enable us to see ourselves but actively to reflect the space around us. If I were to analyse my interest in psychology as a tool, I should say that it certainly isn't about references. Many colleagues work with references in the sense of, say, Pop or Postmodernism, but I just can't. It's somehow against my nature – this constant looking back at the past, like the way I feel about photography.

From what I just said about the performance of people in space you can sense my interest in an *architecture des gestes*, a gestural architecture, as I call it. This is completely different from Pop or Postmodernism; gestural architecture does not appeal so much to memory, knowledge and education, which are central elements of referential architecture. On the contrary, *une architecture des gestes* appeals directly to gestures people understand apart from their education; it appeals to things learned from personal experience, from life experience, from the street, much like the way kids learn.

Louise   You mean, our instinctive gestures?
Jacques   Exactly. I think this instinctive and gestural approach, avoiding any form of reference, is a strong tool, something I wanted

26 *Lego House: One Specific Room*, 'L'Architecture est un jeu ... magnifique', exhibition, Centre Pompidou, Paris, 1985

27 Two photographs of stills from a video filmed inside the *Lego House*

28 Looking out from the Prada Aoyama, Tokyo, towards Miu Miu Aoyama

29 Model of Miu Miu Aoyama showing a section of the polished, mirror-smooth, steel-panelled façade

28

29

to push especially in two recent projects: our Autobahnkirche, a highway chapel in a remote village in the Swiss Alps, and Calder Gardens, a space dedicated to Alexander Calder in downtown Philadelphia.

Louise   I am really interested to hear how much the observation of gestures, movements and subtle signs of people's intuitive behaviour in space plays such a role in your practice. This is fundamentally what we have been working on in most of our films. We very much try to capture people's awareness of their experience of space and time. That's why we often ask ourselves how we can develop that sense of awareness and sensitivity towards space. Our general education, from early childhood, doesn't provide any tool to question how we relate to our surroundings, its qualities, its defects, or even the consciousness of our body in space and all the elements that impact our feelings. Do you think there would be any way we could better develop that collective sensibility to space prior to architecture studies? Could it be a mission of elementary school for instance?

30

Jacques   I haven't thought about it. It could be taught in various ways. Starting in kindergarten, for instance, when kids play around, such as with Lego or doll's houses, which is what I personally loved to do a lot as a child. To have children arrange dolls and furniture, plants and animals differently in space is something you can certainly teach. It is also helpful to walk and talk, describing the things you see on your way, which we did as Lucius Burckhardt's students in the early 1970s. We learned to pay attention – to important but also to unimportant things, such as weeds for example. He called that 'promenadologie'. That was a very healthy experience.

Ila   The way you use mirrors is particularly interesting with respect to this idea of developing more awareness of present time to experience it more consciously. You said that photography is deeply depressing for you because it is bound to memory and nostalgia of a past time, and the mirror is quite the opposite; it's probably the only form of representation which remains in the present, as a living form. It's a surface with no memory and reflects the fleeting present in real time. But more than a representation, it can even be considered a duplication or even a multiplication of space and time in the present, allowing us to intensify our experience of being.

31

Jacques   That's a good point, Ila. Mirrors are about the here and now. And mirrors are not just mirrors. They can be more or less reflective and have different shades of colour. I am thinking of using such a mirror for one of the rooms inside the above-mentioned Autobahnkirche. I am interested in the direct confrontation it will evoke with its *vis-à-vis*. I also like the double connotation mirrors have as something banal and commercial but also as something magic, like the surface of a puddle.

Louise   We wanted to discuss briefly some of your projects that have a more emotional impact than others. Over the years, the work of your office has shown a lot of interest in three kinds of projects that have a great emotional impact: stadiums, museums and care centres. Since antiquity, stadiums have probably always been the emotional spaces *par excellence*, as much as sacred spaces can be, I guess. Knowing your personal interest in football, we can imagine that you design stadiums not only from the perspective of the architect but certainly also from the point of view and experience of the spectator. How much has the spectator in you taught the architect to understand better what a stadium should be?

Ila   Let me just add a brief comment. Most forms of art, like painting, sculpture, literature, are representations of a past emotion or a past event; they share emotion through their representation. In contrast, architecture creates a space to be experienced in the present. The space of a stadium acquires a special existence when all the spectators are together, sharing a collective emotion. The architecture is simply the shell that provides the space for that to happen. Being a football player myself and an enthusiast, I know – in fact, we all know – that a stadium without people is a very nostalgic space, even gloomy I would say. Yet when it is filled with people, it turns into a living organism.

Jacques   As you say, the drama of architecture is that without people nothing works. Crucial to our work is the idea that architecture is a kind of stage for human performance. In a stadium,

45

32

museum, health centre or rehab centre, you need to anticipate that performance. The idea is not to tell people how to behave, but to invite them. Without their involvement, architecture is dead; you get lost, or led astray by other factors like style or references. The question we should really ask is 'How do people perform?' At REHAB Basel, patients may be immobile for weeks so that the ceiling and horizontal views are obviously very important to enrich their perception of nature and the world around them. So that was one important focus in working on that project. When we did the football stadium in Basel, I didn't know of any other stadium that had been designed by an architect; they were always in the hands of contractors. Stadiums have lost their primitive, archaic, powerful, spatial, threatening and frightening qualities, which I particularly love in English stadiums. They used to be ugly, yet extremely impressive. Stadiums in the 1970s were built with these glass ceilings and all this shit that was 'architectural' but had nothing to do with human emotions. I mean as a football player, you're a hardcore fan, and you just want your team to win and the opponents to be scared. So we did everything we could to bring people close to the pitch, to enhance things like sound and colour. These ingredients feed into people's performance. If that succeeds, then these places become architecture; architecture is almost a by-product. For me, there has never been a conflict between understanding the psychology and behaviour of people and my own architectural translation; they have always gone hand in hand. I never saw it as a handicap because I have never been interested in a personal style. If anything, my personal style has always been

33

32 A procession of fans move
    across the landscape towards
    the Allianz Arena, Munich

33 The colour of the stadium's
    luminous body can be changed
    according to which football
    team is playing

this intention to understand where we are, where we go, why we do
what we do. Maybe 'conceptual' is the word to use in this context –
a conceptual approach that has to do with how people perform
and how people behave, which is in turn related to questions of
psychology.

Louise   Could we say that the figure of the architect is related
to the role of the conductor, the *chef d'orchestre d'émotions*, in
some ways?

Jacques   You can make these comparisons, but I don't know …
The conductors I have met have tended to be self-centred, to
believe they were greater than the musicians, greater than the
concert hall, greater even than the composer. You might be right
though. I think the architect is ultimately – I hope this does not sound
hypocritical – not so important. You should just do the job right,
never missing the opportunity to offer the platform to allow people
to do things in their own way. Speaking of stadiums, which are such
a specific form of architecture, every club obviously has its own
tradition but the common denominator for a football stadium is its
hermetic quality. It's like a casserole, it's enclosed. The pressure
grows and is contained. The 'Bird's Nest' is different from all other
stadiums we have done. It's a stadium for athletics, not football.
It has this sense of antiquity with an open sky and a grid, and the
athletes don't compete against each other one-to-one, they're
more of a group. We had to catch a different spirit in the architecture
because after the Olympics were over, it would have to be more
than a monument: it would have to work for the people, to be

47

inviting and appealing and to feel like a park, not like a casserole. Otherwise, it wouldn't have been able to serve other purposes or performances, like marriages or people simply hanging out there. As an architect, my most urgent desire was to design a stadium that could have a post-Olympic life, which meant that it had to be conceived in a completely different way from a football stadium. This is a good example of how an architectural concept is related to an understanding of people's psychology.

Ila   If architecture can be considered as a stage to decipher people's psychology through their behaviours and gestures, do you think the opposite is also true, could architecture also have the power to influence people's collective psychology? To which point can shaping the space of a building, or even a city as a whole, become a powerful or even a dangerous tool?

Jacques   In general, I don't think architecture can proactively change people's collective psychology, except when it is conceived on a large scale under dictatorships, like the Soviet Union, East Germany or in Nazi Germany. Most such ideological architectures were conceived to represent the idea of never-ending power and inspire awe – for example, the Haus der Kunst in Munich, which I revisited recently.

I think buildings can obstruct or inspire public life through the way they are conceived. We opted for the latter when working on Beijing's 'Bird's Nest', which was built at a moment when we were all hoping that China was on the way to becoming a more democratic country. As its nickname suggests, the stadium has been accepted since the beginning, and still now after the Olympic Games, as a place where people like to gather in a friendly way, as in a public park. This is not an ideological piece of architecture but indeed a political one, since the rather iconic grid structure of the building serves as an urban topography for people to gather around and discuss.

34 Andreas Gursky, *Beijing*, 2010. Photograph of the 'Bird's Nest' National Stadium for the 2008 Olympic Games

SPACES OF POTENTIAL

At the opening of Herzog & de Meuron's Battersea campus building for the Royal College of Art (RCA) in the summer of 2022, Jacques Herzog said something deceptively simple and characteristically obtuse: 'You can only see the difference in the context of time when you are looking back.' He may have been referring to the fact that when we discuss the context for architecture, we usually think about topography rather than history. His comment was also a reminder that today's sense of presentism can make it difficult to see the past in its own terms, and the future as a space of potential.

In the case of the RCA's Battersea building, journalists were required to make a leap of the imagination to see the vast, empty, spotlessly clean studios as the hub of creativity that the press release described. But had they returned a few months later, the scene would have looked very different, with ad-hoc temporary walls dividing studios, and an organised mess of student work in progress. As many of the practice's buildings reveal, among them sports stadiums, cultural centres and universities, Herzog & de Meuron's architecture is a stage for people.

The Battersea project marks more than 25 years of Herzog & de Meuron activity in London. In 1996 they won the competition to convert Giles Gilbert Scott's Bankside power station into Tate Modern, which opened as part of the Millennium celebrations in 2000. Laban Dance Centre in Deptford, which combined studios with public facilities, became their second realised London project,

36

37

37 The lawn at Tate Modern
mediates the space of the city
and the transformed building

opening in 2003. Then came a second phase at Tate Modern, the
Blavatnik Building, which was completed in 2016, the year they won
the competition for the new campus building at Battersea. Other
projects in the city include the Serpentine Gallery Pavilion (2012)
and the One Park Drive residential tower in Canary Wharf (2022).

ARCHITECTURE AND SOCIETY
The role of architecture in shaping the activity that takes place
within a building is difficult to assess. A modernist way of thinking
has contributed to the now well-established but technocratic idea
that architects can change society (despite the diminution of
the architectural profession's sense of agency in recent years).
The agency of the public or the occupier tends to be downplayed,
and it is more common these days to see architecture as part of
a process of 'nudging' people into certain behaviours. In the
Anthropocene age, a term popularised by scientists in the 2000s
to denote the era of human influence on the environment, the
agency of people has arguably been relativised even further.
        In this context, Herzog & de Meuron has an unusual angle
on the relationship between architecture and society. Unlike many
contemporary architects, they don't claim their buildings will change
the world or tackle climate change and social inequality. In October
2020, when David Chipperfield wrote an open letter to Jacques
Herzog asking him what architects could do about environmental
catastrophe and poverty, Herzog replied, 'Nothing.' In a disarmingly
honest article, Herzog laid bare the aspirations of the practice,
which are, he wrote, 'to give "utopia" physical shape' and 'respond

to the needs of users'.[1] Herzog & de Meuron are resistant to being labelled according to any philosophy or ideology, but if there is a pervasive strand running through their work, it is a commitment to making spaces for people to 'act'.

ARTISTIC INFLUENCES

The influence of artists rather than other architects has shaped their approach, particularly the strategic thinking embodied by conceptual art. From the beginnings of the practice in 1978, Herzog and Pierre de Meuron were influenced by Donald Judd, having seen his work at the Kunstmuseum Basel in the early 1970s, an interest they shared with their long-term friend and collaborator, the artist Rémy Zaugg. Artistic collaborations, including a brief project with Joseph Beuys in 1978, influenced their early work and particularly their approach to materials, surface and analysis.

Their interest in transformation and perception drew on the work of two artists in particular, Gordon Matta-Clark and Dan Graham, and is described by the practice's long-term chronicler Gerhard Mack.[2] Graham was the subject of a show at the Kunstmuseum Basel in 1996, and a text by Jacques Herzog in the exhibition catalogue [3] commented on the artist's observations of corporate architecture in North America, which Graham noticed had shifted the relationship between public and private space: the large atria of modern office buildings are open to the public and combine extensive glazing and reflections, making people aware of their own presence within a city.

Like a mirrored Dan Graham pavilion which throws attention back onto the viewer, Tate Modern is both an object and a space to explore as an extension of the city. The Turbine Hall is an agora where events, meetings and exhibitions can be held – where people can see and be seen. Similar tactics are deployed at Laban Dance Centre, Prada Aoyama (2003) and Uniqlo Tokyo (2020).

The design of Tate Modern can be seen as a process of cutting away, excavation and opening up – perhaps a reference to Matta-Clark's splitting and cutting of buildings, which was an important influence on Jacques Herzog from the time they both taught at Cornell University in New York in the 1980s. Undoubtedly the most significant of the practice's UK buildings, Tate Modern is the most important project to have emerged from the nation's Millennium celebrations, which included the creation of more than 200 cultural and public commissions. It has become such an essential feature of London since it opened that it is hard to remember the city before it. As a building, it seems to define what is distinctive about London: its past in industry and its future in consumption, culture and leisure. The project was transformational for Herzog & de Meuron, too, and shifted the architects' global profile and their reputation for designing public cultural buildings.

TATE AND THE URBAN RENAISSANCE

Tate Modern is a product of its time: it marked the beginning of the idea that the so-called creative industries are a key component of the British economy, new thinking brought in by Tony Blair's

38

New Labour government soon after its election in 1997. If art and creativity were an industry, we needed buildings on an industrial scale to accommodate them. Tate Modern is also solid evidence of the influence of Richard Rogers's report *Towards an Urban Renaissance* (1999), which advocated urban regeneration based on design excellence.[4]

Features of urban development that transformed London as a whole are key markers of the new urban zone surrounding Tate Modern that since the late 1990s has been named Bankside. These included generous provision of landscaped public space, well-designed infrastructure in the form of transport and pedestrian routes, cultural facilities, cafés and new residential and commercial developments.

The context of time mentioned at the outset is not to downplay Herzog & de Meuron's role in creating Tate Modern, a building they describe as being inspired by the topography of the city. Their architectural interventions treated Gilbert Scott's former power station both as a London monument and an extension of the city's landscape and infrastructure. By removing extraneous structures, they emphasised its monumentality as an object, sitting in an open public space with minimal landscaping. Their interventions highlighted the building's out-of-scale proportions and its sense of otherness within the urban landscape, which seems appropriate given that the surrounding area had originally established itself outside the civilised bounds of the city, as a place where alternative social rules applied and the illegal activities of sixteenth- and seventeenth-century theatres and brothels could be ignored on the other side of the river.

Herzog & de Meuron also opened up an interior that had previously been out of bounds, excavating the basement to create the vast Turbine Hall and creating multiple routes into and through the building, including a ramp as wide as a major road, as if an extension of the City of London's pedways. Sculptural light-boxes make the movement of people on the upper floors visible, giving them priority over the works of art themselves.

41

41 The brickwork of the Blavatnik Building, Tate Modern, London

42 Workshops are the nucleus of activities in the Studio Building at the Royal College of Art's Battersea campus, London

43 Pages 58–59: Street-level access to the Studio Building

In the second phase of Tate Modern, the Blavatnik Building (2016), the architects turned the horizontal city on its side, and made the staircase a twisting route through the vertical landscape – an element that is simultaneously a meeting place and a space for interaction, movement and observation. They described it as 'a vertical city, with squares, streets, lanes and steps'.[5]

Collaboration with an artist was at the heart of Laban Dance Centre in Deptford, a lesser-known but equally thoughtful London project, where the practice worked closely with Michael Craig-Martin RA, initially to develop colour schemes. At Laban, colour is filtered to the outside as washes seen through polycarbonate screens. Craig-Martin was also invited to create murals on the walls of the shared social space, which feature everyday objects linked to the human body, such as clocks, sandals and mirrors. Laban was intended to attract people and to be a public facility, reaching out to Deptford 'like a magnet'[6] and linking the lives of its dancers with the neighbourhood.

INTERIOR PUBLIC SPACE

Herzog & de Meuron employed similar tactics at the new RCA campus in Battersea, where the tarmac road surface is extended through fire-station doors into an unprogrammed, double-height space named the Hangar. Materials and details more associated with the street find their way inside – the tarmac floor, for example, is polished to the degree that it resembles expensive terrazzo. Here, public exhibitions and events reveal the work of students to the city. Around the perimeter of the building, 'shop windows' enable those waiting at bus stops to see into the workshops and studios. Critics have identified a relationship between the RCA building and Tate Modern in their use of brick, but another, perhaps truer relationship is in their creation of interior public space.

Tate Modern ushered in a new era of cultural buildings, not as an example of boosterish iconic architecture, but as an ideal representation of the gallery as a free public space. It offered the possibility of a new type of public building – an alternative to a church or shopping centre – where people could simply exist, experience a sense of collectiveness, or see and be seen.

As if to formalise Tate Modern's offer to the city, in 2021 the Mayor of London Sadiq Khan introduced new planning guidance and a charter that officially designated the interior of certain buildings as 'public space'.[7] Passing without much comment during the Covid-19 pandemic, this could have profound implications for clients and architects, and in the long term will act as a powerful incentive to planners to incorporate public space inside private office buildings. It is a reminder of the work by Dan Graham from the mid-1970s that inspired Herzog & de Meuron to look at cities, although it is also a prompt to consider the meaning of 'public'.

As a building inspired by watching people move around the city, Tate Modern played an important part in the re-categorisation of public and private, and the blurring of boundaries between the two. It was also the first of a series of projects where 'the city became the model for individual buildings'. A commitment to public, unprogrammed space is something the practice has brought to bear in many subsequent projects around the world, including the Walker Art Center, Minneapolis, completed in 2005, the Elbphilharmonie, Hamburg (2016) and the M+ museum of visual culture, Hong Kong (2021).

A year after the opening of Tate Modern, Herzog & de Meuron was awarded the Pritzker Prize for Architecture. Receiving the award, Jacques Herzog said, 'Architecture can only survive as architecture in its physical and central diversity and not as a vehicle for ideology of some kind.' There is a core humanist principle at the heart of Herzog & de Meuron: a commitment to the city, to social life and to the users of buildings.

DIFFERENT TAKES

Herzog & de Meuron: Architecture and Perception

44 Stills from the 1995 film
Anpassung und Setzung
(*Conformity and Challenge*)
by Ulrich Gambke of Jacques
Herzog commenting on the
prefabricated elements of
1950s generic housing
during a stroll through Basel

A film shot by Ulrich Gambke[1] in 1994 of a young Jacques Herzog strolling through 1950s housing highlights two important, very different takes on architecture. In a still from the film, Herzog is seen standing in front of a façade, gazing at it; another shows him walking between buildings.[2] In the arrested shots architecture becomes a picture, a view with symbolic meaning. By contrast, in the moving images architecture reveals its volumes, its tactile capacity to occupy space and create space. And those spaces are continually reconfigured by the human being walking through the site, showing that space only fully evolves through movement.

That at least is how Michel de Certeau described it in 1980 in connection with his perception of a particular city, *the* modernist city: New York.[3] Looking down from the Twin Towers, from on high, taking in a godlike, all-embracing view from above, it seems to him as if the city has a particular texture; it turns into a physical fabric, a text demanding to be read and deciphered. It becomes a stage constructed from concrete, steel and glass, filled with signs of excessive production and extravagance that are only perceived from up there, from afar, through the sense of sight alone. But that kind of all-encompassing view is not available to the pedestrians down below. Day-to-day life sends people out into the city and they engage with it in myriad ways, with many knowing it like the backs of their hands. Daily excursions – were we to plot their ins and outs on an imaginary map – do not form smooth, easily read surfaces. Walking, be it with a destination or quite aimless, is as much about exploring space as it is about generating space, and it involves the whole body with all its various modes of perception, which in turn bring out the haptic and tactile qualities of that space, its acoustic and olfactory properties.

Architecture, each individual building, is both part of the fabric of the city and an intervention into it. Architecture directs a person's footsteps, their movements, their perceptions in the city; at the same time it is itself determined by pre-empted, literally foreseen, imagined movements and perceptions that take place within and with it. Above all, each architectural façade provides a picture, a signal that tells not only of the functions and ideals of building but also of the ways materials have been and still are used. Buildings, as volumetric bodies, obstruct the people walking round or into them, using them yet ignoring them.

Different takes on architecture have different histories. Baroque architecture was all about visual impact, about a sweeping, picturesque view that unfolded before the very eyes of the astounded onlooker, representing the dignity and status of its owner. In contrast to the Baroque with all its splendour, Modernism developed residential architecture on the basis of the way rooms were to be distributed and used, separating and/or connecting the occupants.[4] Routes predetermined by passages and doors have social consequences: they facilitate or prevent encounters, they exclude or include, they open up shared spaces or they shield a private place of retreat from curious outsiders. In modern life, routes and paths shape the perception of architecture, both inside and as it is seen from outside. A building's exterior – according to an important modernist ideology – reflects its function.

Herzog & de Meuron's work is nurtured and inspired by the different ways built structures are perceived. And they expose the ideology of 'form follows function' as such – as an ideology – by complicating the question of function, in the sense that 'function' is not solely restricted to potential uses. The task of architecture, at least in Herzog & de Meuron's view, is also to serve as a repository for memories and to absorb its location and surroundings into its own structures and forms. At the same time, the surroundings are changed by this morphological intervention and by the materials used for a building, which subsequently come into their own, be it in harmony or at odds with the location.

It therefore does not come as a surprise that some of Herzog & de Meuron's most important commissions have been for archives and storage facilities or display spaces. One early commission in particular, which catapulted the office onto the international architectural stage, exemplifies the way that memories, function and the latter's visible manifestation can interconnect in their architecture. In 1987 they completed a fully automated warehouse for Ricola, renowned makers of herbal cough drops and candies. The building looks like a hermetic, layered block, a coherent entity that gives visible form to both its function, as a storage facility, and to structures seen in the local landscape, such as the limestone quarry within which it is situated and the stacks of planks at the sawmills that abound in the area. The viewer is also struck by the building's inaccessibility, which has an almost physical impact, for the eye is unable to penetrate the layered block, which is not pierced by even a single window. Just one, seemingly tiny door – pushed right into one corner – hints at the presence of human beings moving in and around the building. And the presence of human beings is very much felt in the notion of stacking and storing that is implicit in the exterior of the warehouse – an activity that connects the people who work here with the landscape around them.

The interaction of diverse elements, human and non-human agents, materials and tools, ideas and uses, actions and perceptions all (as the British anthropologist Timothy Ingold has put it) contribute to the quality of a dwelling.[5] 'Dwelling' is not used here in its narrower sense, as a private living space. Ingold uses it in a wider sense to refer to 'a way of being at home in the world',[6] with architecture providing a literal and metaphorical shell. He thus abandoned a longstanding distinction: between inventive, self-aware human architects building according to some conceptual principle, and animals acting on instinct, beholden to their physical make-up and needs, building structures without the benefit of 'design' skills.

45

45 Schaulager, Laurenz Foundation,
Münchenstein/Basel

In Ingold's view a building is not just a container that is designed, erected and ultimately inhabited and lived in. It is only in the fluid interplay of materials, tools, uses and perceptions, building materials and the location, that architecture emerges as 'dwellings', as a lived-in, liveable world shaped by its inhabitants; in return, that same architecture configures its occupants' routes, behaviours and forms of communication. Seemingly static architecture thus comes to embody processes of perception, usage and the symbolic and actual occupation of places and spaces. Living, Ingold has said, is movement. Dwellings, as shells and as the expression of this movement, are living organisms, and architectural form is the outcome of a wide variety of processes.

At the sight of an aerial shot of Herzog & de Meuron's converted Turbine Hall at Tate Modern in London, completed in 2000, Jacques Herzog remarked in an interview for the programme *Sternstunde Philosophie* on Swiss Radio and Television (SRF) that this was not the best way to view the building, because the visitor's perception of it was very different.[7] Anyone approaching the Turbine Hall at ground level, looking up at it, is confronted with its monumental size and weight, whereas the view from above creates a controlling, diminishing perception. Herzog & de Meuron have frequently pointed out that their own view of the built world has primarily been shaped by film and photography. The distance created by the eye of the camera causes architecture to recede, as it were, allowing a building's most striking features to come to

46

the fore. So, different takes on architecture can be reinforced by the nature of its presentation: am I viewing it from a distance, as a pictorial, semiotic phenomenon, or am I moving through spaces it has opened up or generated, highlighting the unfinishable processes of a living organism?

The Royal Academy show explores how architecture can be exhibited in keeping with the conditions of its perception, and how the processual nature of building and the multiplicity of its uses and functions can be conveyed. Display cases house models, case studies and the results of investigations into a huge range of materials and technologies alongside Thomas Ruff's large-format photographs of buildings by the studio. A new film focuses on the REHAB Basel convalescent home, built just over twenty years ago. The process of designing and making is revealed in an in-depth study of part of a new medical facility in Zurich, demonstrating the practice's interest in new technologies and its endless ability to adapt to the demands of the present.

46 Thomas Ruff, *Haus Nr. 4 II (Ricola Laufen)*, 1991. Photograph of the Ricola Storage Building, Laufen, Switzerland

47

ENVISIONING UNIMAGINABLE ARCHITECTURE

A Filmmaker's Perspective

47 Thomas Ruff, *Hongkong*, 2009. Photograph of the Tai Kwun – Centre for Heritage and Arts, Hong Kong

When masterfully executed, film and architecture intersect when they invite the onlooker on an emotional journey that they will hold in their memories forever. Personally, it doesn't matter to me if it's a house, library, museum or a film; if I am moved emotionally, the art form has a profound effect on my subconscious inspiration. It raises the bar and expands my brain to believe there are more ways to learn, experience and grow.

One of my most vivid memories is of visiting the Herzog & de Meuron office in Basel for the first time. I was overcome not only by the pure innovative horizon, but by their genius, their artistry as architects who have envisioned unimaginable creations. On one hand, I was infinitely inspired, but upon reflection I felt the urgent need to work harder and more vigilantly to become the best storyteller I could be. I was awestruck by their ability to co-create in harmony with the elements at their disposal. Their work never seems meant to be simply structures of stone, wood, metal, concrete, etc. arranged in a pleasing fashion; with the use of light and colour, their buildings tell stories, represent characters and establish dialogue. The result is a timeless artistic achievement.

I was incredibly fortunate to grow up with a mother who enforced the importance of space, light and the absence of light. From a very early age her influence allowed me to recognise how these elements work in tandem to affect one's emotional well-being. When I conceptualise my vision for a film, I of course imagine the formation of characters and soundscapes, but the aspects that really define the transition from script to screen are the colour, light, architecture and design. These are the core principles for my visualisation of any story.

The sensations we experience when watching a film directly correlate with the seen versus the unseen. Our emotions about a shot are defined by light. Through the light, shadows are illuminated as they belong to one another. What we observe and feel becomes its own consciousness as a living being. While playing with the power of the unseen, the measurable becomes immeasurable.

Another key factor of the emotional language of storytelling is perspective. When making a film, by utilising the elements of the story I'm in complete control of what I want the spectator to feel at any given moment. As a filmmaker I have the luxury, unlike an architect, of being able to highlight or hide what I believe serves the story within the frame. For example, I can show a door, but the camera never has to reveal what is behind it. Architects don't have that freedom, they are forced to show you what's behind the door. On top of that, they are restricted by gravity, engineering and their commissioners' specific requirements. This is why I think of architects as magicians, and architecture as their form of magic.

I puzzle over how the plans were constructed and how they all took shape. Herzog & de Meuron consistently operate at a heightened level of excellence and I'm still trying to glimpse behind the curtain to see how their magic is distilled.

Both architecture and storytelling originate from putting pen to paper. Drawing and writing are the beginning of visualisation in both expressions. Most screenplays follow a three-act structure and dive into the who, what, where, when and why, as well as theme and suspense. Similarly, when I enter one of their buildings, I always feel I am being invited into one of Herzog & de Meuron's stories. As I walk deeper into the space, the details of a secondary storyline are revealed. It's fascinating how in architecture, space changes with the influence of light and colour; depending on the time of day, one can have a completely different emotional experience in the space. The story is often also told through negative space, which I love to utilise in movies. Negative space creates tension and curiosity, and when I leave Herzog & de Meuron's buildings, it's like I'm walking out of the final scene of an Alfred Hitchcock movie; the suspense has passed.

Hitchcock was one of the first filmmakers who understood the power of architecture, using different environments for perspectival shifts and tension. He carefully planned out interiors and exteriors, thoughtfully designing his shots and incorporating all details of architecture to get the most tension out of a scene. Architecture was a blueprint incorporated into the psychological texture of his films. There are many examples of this throughout his body of work, for instance in *Psycho* the composition of the sets reflects the split personality of the lead character Norman Bates: the deteriorated house on the hill stands in opposition to the rectilinear shape of the motel. This serves as a visual representation of Norman's mental state as he struggles to find his identity.

Another director who explored architecture's juxtaposition with nature was Michelangelo Antonioni. There is often tension in his films between the written word and the image, mankind and the environment, his final dichotomy lying between being and nothingness. Architecture can be approached through both its intrinsic and extrinsic perspectives, and this is how Antonioni brought his frames to life. With calculated movements within precisely calibrated spaces, he creates an emotional and existential ambiguity, using architectural elements to penetrate his audiences' inner psyche.

Herzog & de Meuron permeate our consciousness in a similar way, using metaphors and symbols of both the future and the past – like an inorganic representation of an organic creation. I hear the symphonies they have composed in their buildings – different tunes and soundscapes dependent on the space. Filmmaking is a fluid art-form that distinguishes itself by its constant creation of forms and imagery. Emotions are often expressed directly, given form through sound, dialogue and visual storytelling. The dialogue can guide and direct like a crutch. Achieving that unspoken word in architecture is one of the most difficult ways to communicate a story, but somehow Herzog & de Meuron are repeatedly able to do

48

this and more, seemingly finding more complexity in the simplicity with which they distil their vision. For me this is the highest form of communication in art; their language evolves more towards abstraction, to what is truly essential.

This essentiality unveils a poetry, each building in itself becoming standalone verse, an interplay between the architecture and its creators. What forges this dynamic relationship? Where does it conflict and where does it cohere, or is it a constant flux of all the elements Herzog & de Meuron choose to engage with? As a filmmaker I try to make the invisible visible, the hidden manifest – to use allegorical ways to express my vision and to spark emotion. Similarly in Herzog & de Meuron's architecture, layers of experience are conveyed through emotions recollected in tranquillity. Structure and image collide to provoke thought and emotion – the ultimate goal of all creation. Herzog & de Meuron constantly eclipse expectations, challenging themselves by adding a whole new set of complex ideas to each new project. They are destined to surprise, innovate and levitate the architectural narrative for many years to come.

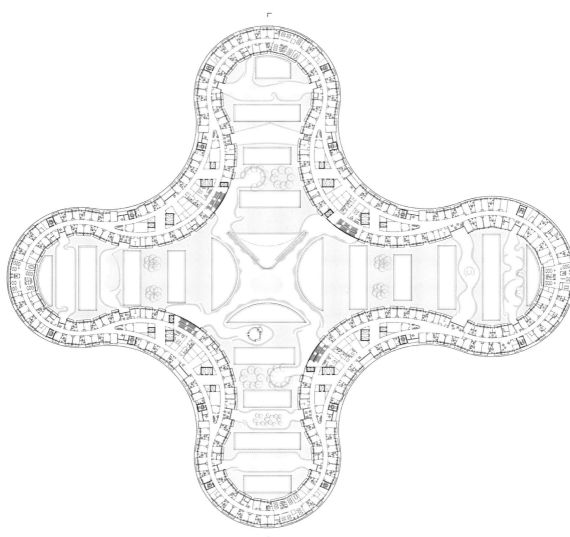

49

BUILDING FOR MORE THAN HEALTHCARE

49 Plan of Level 2 for the New North Zealand Hospital in Hillerød, Denmark, showing the arrangement of wards forming the perimeter of the large central garden

As a Dane, you should occasionally tear yourself away from the plain and seek out mountains, train yourself to have vision and dizziness[1]

These words of the well-known Danish poet Benny Andersen (1929–2018) formed a framework for the way my close working relationship with Herzog & de Meuron began. In them, Andersen both captures the soul of the Danish people and challenges the 'Laws of Jante' – a set of unwritten, egalitarian principles ingrained in Danish and Nordic society that frown upon non-conformity and personal ambition.

When I was appointed in late 2011 to establish a body to plan a new super-hospital north of Copenhagen, I found the Laws of Jante weighing me down and pushing me to conform. Hospitals today are some of the strongest markers of our welfare society. They exemplify civilisation and cohesion. At that time fifteen other hospital projects were already underway in Denmark as part of a €6 billion project to modernise the country's national healthcare system; our New North Zealand Hospital (NNZ) at Hillerød was to be the sixteenth and last of these. The new hospital site was a pristine meadow and wetland that was beautiful but also challenging. The area is known for its protected species, of which more than 1,500 were transferred to a safe location.

Intuition told me that Hillerød was a unique opportunity to be curious, and to create a new sort of hospital. So I assembled a team consisting primarily of people with backgrounds in behavioural and human sciences. This instantly set thoughts and dialogues in motion. Architects, anthropologists and sociologists talked to doctors, nurses and patients, and pretty quickly we involved thought-leaders and leaders from other fields. If we were to understand the health needs of the future, we would have to *seek out mountains*. It would not be enough just to build a new hospital or *sygehus* (literally 'sick-house': the word's pejorative connotations alone left it far from our transformative vision).

It was clear from our first field studies and from visits to hospitals built in the late 1990s and early 2000s in neighbouring countries and across the Atlantic that distinct typologies existed with an *institutional* understanding, both in terms of the way hospitals were organised, and in their architecture, décor and mindset. I was not a qualified health professional, let alone a 'system native', and my humility perhaps enabled me to challenge the system and the experts who represent it. Healthcare is of course scientifically driven, with treatments and care based on evidence and constantly developing research. But when it comes to hospital architecture, perhaps surprisingly, such an approach is

71

50

less prevalent: certified health architects say there is a certain way to do it but the evidence to support this is often missing.

When we started our planning as the client, we immediately questioned this institutional understanding of what a hospital is. We needed a new definition of a hospital as a welfare building. A place that understands and respects humanity and dignity. Professionals. Patients. Relatives. Citizens. We formulated various taglines to emphasise the project's ambitions: 'beyond bricks', 'a blank canvas', 'a hospital that doesn't feel like a hospital'.

Our ambition was thus to reinvent the hospital typology. We moved back in time and looked at hospital gardens and Le Corbusier's unrealised 1965 plan for a hospital in Venice, with its horizontal focus and four levels. We wanted to escape the prevailing verticality of healthcare, with its emphasis on isolated departments, and to promote a more horizontal model, very adaptable, in which care would be integrated and focused on the patient. And we wanted to take an even more radical step: our hospital would be a gathering place for the local community, a place where you might

50 The New North Zealand
    Hospital is an undulating
    horizontal building connected
    to the landscape

meet to go for a walk. We engaged the founding director of Tate Modern in London, Lars Nittve, to lead the art programme of the project, to make it relevant. Lars shortlisted artists of the highest international calibre – Roman Signer, James Turrell, Maya Lin, Pipilotti Rist, Susan Philipsz – to develop works to complement the hospital and invite visitors who had no 'hospital purpose', to be inspired, illuminated, distracted and to be together.

This foresight is part of a broader vision in which the hospital building itself is seen as a bridge to a better healthcare approach. The challenge is to build for the role that hospitals will have in the future, while simultaneously bringing that future into the present. We envisioned a model in which the hospital is one node in a larger continuum of care. This model emphasises outpatient therapy over inpatient care, mental health, healing as a process that is most effective at home, virtual consultations, and opportunities for communities to become partners in caring for the sick. In a sense, the goal was to deinstitutionalise and transform the hospital from a place where the ill come and stay, into a place where care

is centralised but connected with the community outside. We believe we have gone beyond a mere hospital building.

When you know that a hospital is primarily active between 8 am and 4 pm on weekdays, and that loneliness is one of the biggest health challenges, you ask yourself to expand your understanding of the structure. To imagine an assembly hall or a community centre, a place of education, a community kitchen, art and culture as common denominators. We imagined a hospital that would not feel like a hospital. Our dialogues with foundations and grass-roots organisations supported this aspiration. To make such initiatives sustainable, you need mobilisation, determined people and high-quality solutions able to withstand the scrutiny of the news media.

We explained to the politicians that it would be wise on a greenfield site like Hillerød to do something modest. They agreed. We presented them with a shortlist of top architectural firms who had not participated in hospital projects but whom we considered capable of finding a new interpretation of a hospital at Hillerød. At the head of our shortlist was the practice from Basel. After several constructive dialogues, the politicians gave us permission to contact Herzog & de Meuron (and two other architects, besides the four pre-qualified teams). We did so as soon as we had completed our competition brief, and they invited us to visit Basel.

This was the starting point of our collaboration with Herzog & de Meuron. We got in touch with them, visited their REHAB Basel clinic (2002; extension 2020) and discussed how to arrive at a hospital concept that would fulfil our ambitions.

Herzog & de Meuron's reputation among Danish architects is considerable. Since the 1990s, their work has been a regular feature on the curriculum of the Royal Danish Academy of Fine Arts in Copenhagen. They do not merely replicate the past. They live life

52

ahead of most of us. They interpret, experiment, challenge. They are uncompromising. But behind their method lies an unusually gifted and curious approach. Their team of skilled, responsive and cosmopolitan staff and associates brings a freshness and timelessness to the solutions they create. Not only do they build on their practice's forty-plus years of history and experience, they also add new layers through structured research, precise methodology and the insights they gain from their many projects.

When you arrive at Herzog & de Meuron's campus at Rheinschanze 6 and enter through their perforated copper gate, a very special world opens up. The combination of richness of detail and simplicity would fascinate any architecture lover, but what is most striking is the spirit that permeates the place. A mixture of individual and collective dedication stands out, in specific projects at different stages of maturity, in prototypes and in various test solutions for façades, components and perspectives. The practice is a workshop, a laboratory and a faculty. Everyone has a well-defined role and a sense of responsibility. It is clear and discreet. Subdued and understated. Self-aware and humble. The ideal environment for thinking about reinventing the hospital model.

The task of making buildings all over the world for prominent and well-known clients and institutions can be achieved only with clear management structures and an exceptionally skilled staff. During my years of collaboration with Herzog & de Meuron, I have been determined to see as much of their architecture as I can, in order to understand their thinking and the practice's culture. During travels and vacations, I visited their buildings throughout Europe, the US and Asia, and I met their local employees and talked about the thinking behind and the process of making each one. All projects have some history, of course, but I was struck constantly by how polite, accommodating and gifted their representatives were, and how pronounced was their knowledge of the world, science, culture and art. These were Renaissance people who could explain unpretentiously and at a specialist level subjects as diverse as geology, social conditions, art and engineering. This level of expertise is evident throughout the practice's portfolio, which experiments, adds to existing layers of knowledge, explores and moves easily between the big and the bold and the small and the everyday, as much as between disciplines.

When our collaboration with Herzog & de Meuron gained momentum with the publication of their winning proposals in April 2014, we started exchanging inspirations and books we had enjoyed. We made sightseeing and restaurant recommendations and spent time getting to know one another. We talked together. During the two-phase competition, Herzog & de Meuron, the only non-Danish architectural team, interpreted the Danish architectural tradition in a gentle, functional and forward-looking way. They drew inspiration from the landscape architect Carl Theodor Sørensen's allotment gardens at Naerum and the Louisiana Museum of Modern Art. Great architecture is inclusive and uncompromising at the same time – in order to last. Herzog & de Meuron made the 124,000-square-metres building for Hillerød human and intimate, both inviting and present, never forgetting that it must also function as a place of treatment. Short distances, large medical units, logistics. Human life. And fate.

Their design was everything we as the client had hoped for, and more. Four symmetrical lobes curve around a landscaped campus and a vast interior courtyard. This plan brings together the seemingly contradictory needs of a large central garden and the necessity for short internal connections. The building is only four storeys tall. The lower two floors are dedicated to examination and treatment, and the upper two are patient wards. Unlike most modern hospitals, in which departments occupy their own floors, the horizontal planning of the North New Zealand Hospital puts its specialists alongside one another. Patient rooms are intimate and cosy, with a focus on privacy, with windows and balconies providing views to the nearby forest or into the gardens in the courtyard. The building symbolised a breakthrough in healing architecture Horizontal, human, organic and playful, intuitive and flexible, respectful, and functional wherever required. Despite its substantial size and its idiosyncratic, distinct form, the building is unexpectedly non-monumental and approachable. A pavilion in the woods.

Although ambitious, the same concept appears in the detailing as much as in the hospital's structure. Herzog & de Meuron made use of many natural materials such as wood, and added elements such as carefully detailed ceilings, remembering that patients in hospital beds spend most of their time looking upwards. They also incorporated custom-made, almost domestic elements that further deinstitutionalise the hospital and align with the emerging shift in today's healthcare to bring certain treatments into homes. Their aim always was to humanise the hospital and to destigmatise the experience of being ill.

Our collaboration with Herzog & de Meuron was a long-term one carried forward by openness, respect, ambition and curiosity. And, from my side, tenacity. Any client for a large public project must deal with a legion of stakeholders and interests.

53

53 Aerial view of the hospital
under construction

Some considerations are barely rational but they must all be
taken into account, so as to find a way through the swirling current
of finances, risk, functionality, public expectation and the common,
long-term ambitions that we shared with Herzog & de Meuron.
Over the years, this led to disagreements, and to moments when
co-operation intensified and muscles in both camps had to be
flexed. All part of the game, of course, and though these situations
are sometimes painful, our mutual trust and a common history led
to their resolution. It was a cornerstone of our collaboration that
Herzog & de Meuron maintained a consistent core team of three
to five architects who were involved throughout the entire project.
This provided not only an insight into decisions along the way, but
also, and more importantly, created a sense of identity and
ownership. Both are crucial when setting new standards.

In many ways our ambition to rethink healthcare tended
towards the visionary, despite also being a necessity. And it was
closely linked to our intimate partnership with Herzog & de Meuron.
I'm not an architect, although I am married to one. We shared
ambitions, understood aspirations and completely unwrapped
the problem. Given the right circumstances, Herzog & de Meuron
can influence the way we experience public spaces – the way
we perceive them and the way we behave in them with each other.
Their practice's contribution to healthcare is significant, because
their intrinsic characteristic is the space in which we almost feel
out of balance and dizzy. Herzog & de Meuron know how to create
real, transformative buildings.

RICOLA-EUROPE SA
PRODUCTION AND STORAGE BUILDING

MULHOUSE-BRUNSTATT, FRANCE
PROJECT: 1992
REALISATION: 1993

The building's form (overleaf) resembles a cardboard box with open flaps. The cantilevered roofs on its two long sides create shade and shelter for deliveries. Inside, light is filtered through translucent polycarbonate façade panels with a repeating silkscreened plant motif based on photographs by Karl Blossfeldt.

'We wanted an image that related to the garden outside, but that was not too naturalistic. The effect of the image in repetition was crucial; the one we chose was still recognisable as a plant, but the repetition also turned it into something different, transforming the commonplace into something new.'
Jacques Herzog
Founder

EBERSWALDE TECHNICAL SCHOOL LIBRARY

EBERSWALDE, GERMANY
PROJECT: 1994–96
REALISATION: 1997–99

The prefabricated concrete panels that clad the building's exterior are an adaptation of the sgraffito technique, where images, silkscreened onto concrete using a cure-retardant liquid instead of ink, are revealed in the contrast between smooth and rough surfaces.

'We invited the artist Thomas Ruff to make a selection of motifs from a visual diary of newspaper photographs related to the arts, history, politics and science he has been compiling since 1981. He proceeded from the principle that a library is a public building "to develop historical and social awareness".'
Pierre de Meuron
Founder

DOMINUS WINERY

YOUNTVILLE, NAPA VALLEY, CALIFORNIA, USA
PROJECT: 1995
REALISATION: 1996–98

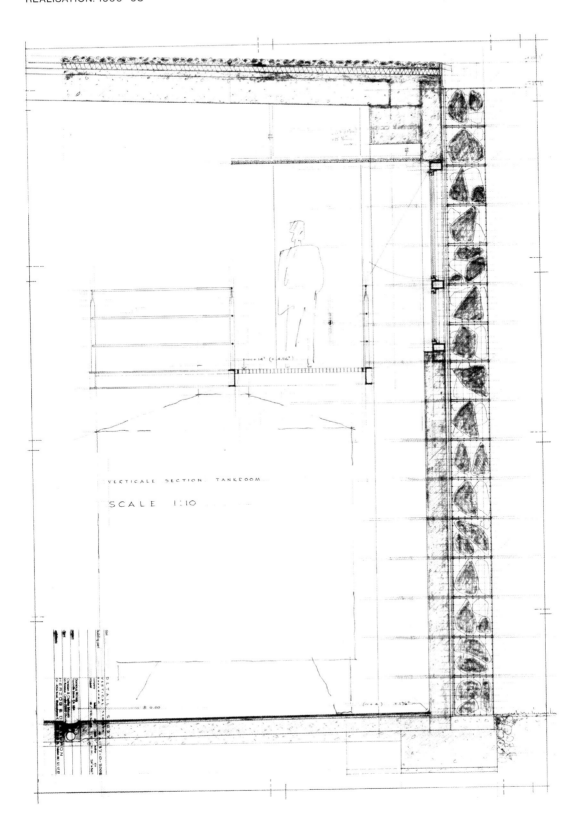

VERTICALE SECTION TANKROOM

SCALE 1:10

The winery bridges the main axis of the vineyard. Often used in river engineering, gabions (wire containers filled with stones) form an inert mass to insulate the building against heat by day and cold by night – a passive climatisation approach to reduce energy consumption using natural materials. Local basalt in the gabions ranges from dark green to black, and allows the building to blend in beautifully with its landscape.

'Depending on where you look from or how close you stand to the wall, it seems either hermetic like concrete or transparent like lace. The gap between the stones is as relevant as the stones themselves.'
Jacques Herzog
Founder

LABAN DANCE CENTRE

DEPTFORD, LONDON, UK
COMPETITION: 1997
PROJECT: 1998–99
REALISATION: 2000–03

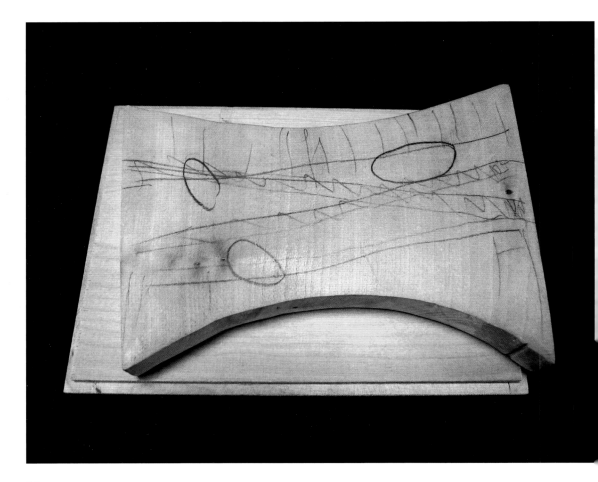

The curved embrace of the façade consists of glass and polycarbonate panels, transparent or translucent depending on whether the space behind them requires a view, and also on environmental needs (sun, glare, heat and energy). A colour scheme designed with artist Michael Craig-Martin determines the rhythm and orientation both inside and outside the building.

'The interior is organised like a village, with courtyards and streets, an inner topography similar to that of REHAB Basel which was designed around the same time.'
Christine Binswanger
Senior Partner

SCHAULAGER, LAURENZ FOUNDATION

MÜNCHENSTEIN/BASEL, SWITZERLAND
PROJECT: 1998–99
REALISATION: 2000–03

The Schaulager is a new building type, a structure in which art is stored but remains accessible for the public to view. Works are displayed closer together than in a museum, taking up considerably less space. The architecture expresses its storage function with heavy solid outer walls that provide support and massive inertia, rising in layers to reveal the fluvial gravel excavated during construction.

'For the windows, we realised that the conventional right-angled shape wouldn't do. Experiments with crushed metal cylinders pressed into plaster slabs looked like cracks in the earth. The resulting windows seem like natural processes but are actually calculated forms made with digital tools.'
Jacques Herzog
Founder

PRADA AOYAMA

TOKYO, JAPAN
PROJECT: 2000–02
REALISATION: 2001–03

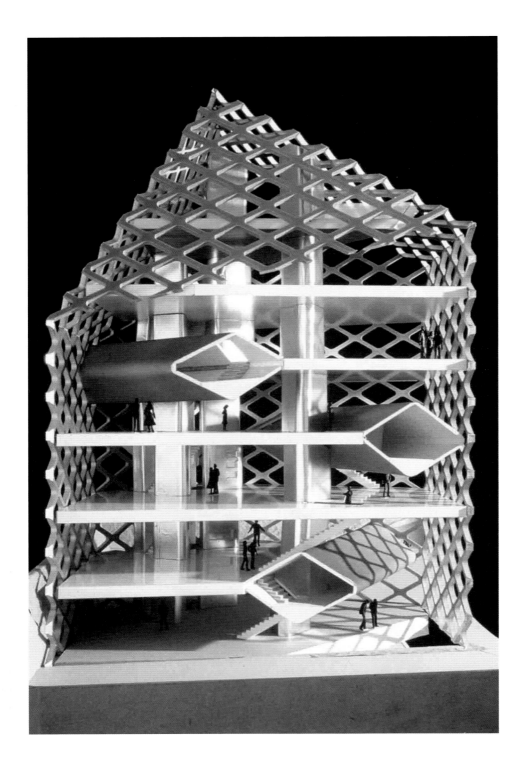

The façade's rhomboid-shaped grid is clad with a combination of convex, concave or flat glass panels. These differing geometries generate faceted reflections, enabling visitors to see constantly changing, almost cinematographic perspectives of Prada products, the city and themselves.

'Structure, space and façade form a single unit in this building. The vertical cores, the horizontal tubes, the floor slabs and the façade grid define the space but, at the same time, they are the structure and the façade.'
Stefan Marbach
Senior Partner

NATIONAL STADIUM
MAIN STADIUM FOR THE 2008 OLYMPIC GAMES

BEIJING, CHINA
COMPETITION: 2002–03
PROJECT: 2003–05
REALISATION: 2003–08

As one approaches the 'Bird's Nest' (its nickname coined by the Chinese themselves), the stadium's geometrically clear-cut and rational overall configuration of lines separates out into huge, distinct components. Almost like an artificial forest, this chaotic thicket of supports, beams and stairs – façade, structure, ornament and public space all in one – encircles the stadium.

'A stadium is different from other building types. It is much rougher and based on a few strong ideas. We learned that lesson working on other stadiums like the Allianz Arena in Munich. The way people behave in them is entirely different than in a museum or a store. In addition, a stadium is utterly different in scale: it is more like a collective vessel or, in Beijing, like a public artificial landscape.'
Tobias Winkelmann
Associate Partner

'We were not simply interested in the Olympics but much more in the everyday life that would follow. The Piranesian lattice that surrounds the seating was conceived as a large public sculpture, designed to attract the people of Beijing. Like a park, a recreational area where people can gather and do things together. Which actually ties in with social conventions in China.'
Jacques Herzog
Founder

ELBPHILHARMONIE HAMBURG

HAMBURG, GERMANY
CONCEPT: 2001–03
PROJECT: 2004–14
REALISATION: 2006–16

This harbourside complex accommodates a concert hall, a hall for chamber music, restaurants, bars, a panoramic terrace, apartments, a hotel and parking facilities. These varied uses are combined in one building as they would be in a city. At its heart is the main concert hall that places audiences and musicians in the foreground to such an extent that, together, the people determine the space.

'We looked for a design that would unite three different spatial experiences: the ancient Greek amphitheatre carved out of stone cliffs, the verticality and relationship between the performers and audience of Shakespeare's theatre and contemporary football stadiums, and finally the marquee or festival tent.'
Jacques Herzog
Founder

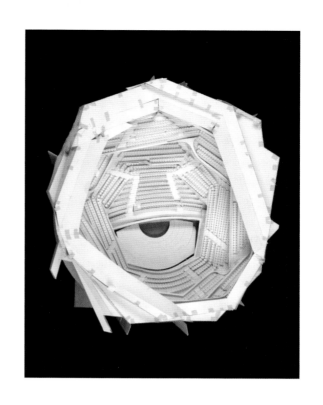

'The Elbphilharmonie marks a location that most people in Hamburg know about but have never really noticed. The new building has been extruded from the shape of Kaispeicher A, a brick warehouse built in 1966. However, the top and bottom of the new structure are entirely different. In contrast to the quiet, plain warehouse, the broad, undulating sweep of the roof rises as an expression of reaching out into new territory, into the harbour area along the shores of the River Elbe.'
Ascan Mergenthaler
Senior Partner

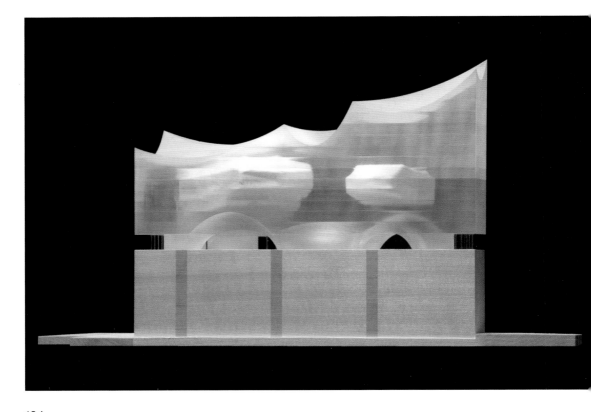

TATE MODERN

LONDON, UK

FIRST PHASE:
COMPETITION: 1994–95
PROJECT: 1995–97
REALISATION: 1998–2000

SECOND PHASE:
COMPETITION: 2005
PROJECT: 2005–12
REALISATION: 2010–16

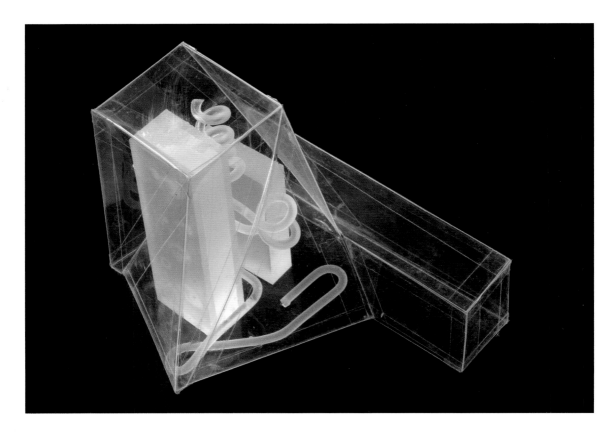

Tate Modern has changed London since it first opened in 2000, impacting the city's urban design and its artistic, cultural and social life. The later addition of the Blavatnik Building, completed in 2016, combined elements of the old and new, to be expressed as a whole and to function as a single organism. Using the existing palette of brick in a radical new way, the perforations in the brickwork (overleaf) transform it from a solid, massive outer layer covering the building's concrete skeleton into a delicate veil. The continuous wrap is broken by horizontal cuts that allow views and provide daylight and natural ventilation to internal spaces.

'The extension provides a range of diverse public spaces dedicated to rest and reflection, making and doing, group learning and private study. These spaces are spread across the new structure and linked by a generous public stair rising through the building. The vertical path of spaces is as clear as the horizontal orientation evident in the first building transformation.'
Ascan Mergenthaler
Senior Partner

1111 LINCOLN ROAD

MIAMI BEACH, FLORIDA, USA
PROJECT: 2005–08
REALISATION: 2008–10

Here, the structure is the architecture. 1111 Lincoln Road comprises an existing building, car parking, retail, restaurants and a private residence. A family of exposed concrete slabs, precisely positioned as floor plates, columns and ramps, are a result of a complex overlapping of car movement, site and building requirements.

'The simple idea of adding floor height to some levels makes them attractive for other uses beyond just parking: workouts, yoga, parties, photo- and film shoots, fashion shows, concerts and other social activities take place at 1111 on a regular basis. Although privately owned, the building is like an extension of the public street.'
Jason Frantzen
Senior Partner

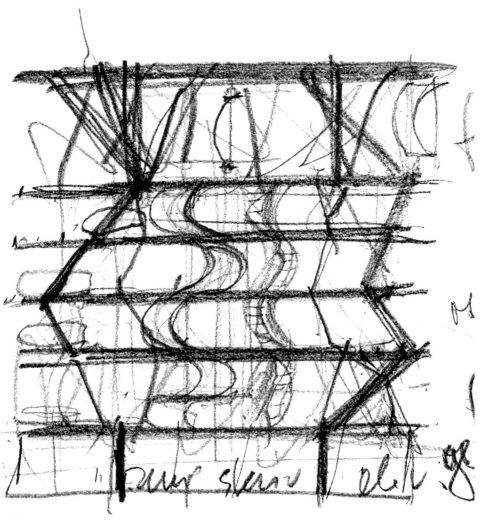

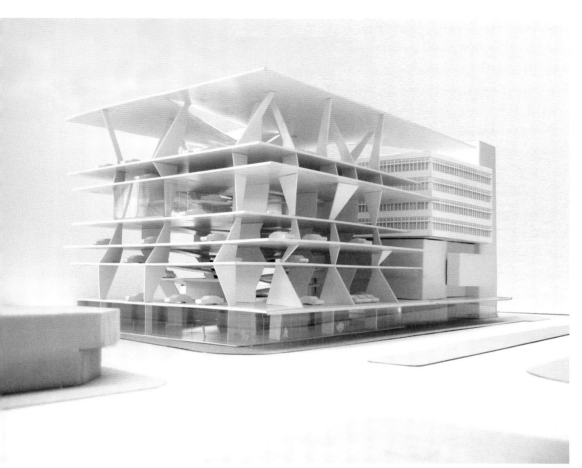

VITRAHAUS

VITRA CAMPUS,
WEIL AM RHEIN, GERMANY
PROJECT: 2006–09
REALISATION: 2007–09

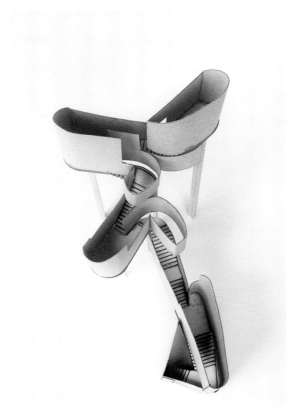

The VitraHaus shows furniture and objects for the home in an environment suited to their character and use. Simple house shapes are stacked, extruded and pressed – mechanical procedures used in industrial production – to become complex configurations in space, merging outside and inside with surprising transitions and views of the landscape.

'A sequence of staircases creates special places and specific routes for people to walk through the stack of houses – not only individuals but also schools, families and tour groups. But we never expected this showroom to become such a popular weekend destination, like a museum.'
Pierre de Meuron
Founder

56 LEONARD STREET

NEW YORK CITY, USA
PROJECT: 2006–08, 2012–17
REALISATION: 2008, 2012–17

56 Leonard Street acts against the anonymity and repetitiveness of residential towers. Despite its great size, the tower's ambition is to achieve a character that expresses the individuality, even intimacy, of housing. It is designed from the inside out as a stack of rooms, each unique and identifiable within the whole, where only five of the 145 apartments are repeated.

'The tower is very much a result of accepting and pushing to the limit simple and familiar local methods of construction. It shows its structural "bones" rather than hiding beneath layers of cladding. The building has extreme proportions at the very edge of what is structurally possible.'
Ascan Mergenthaler
Senior Partner

ARENA DO MORRO

MÃE LUIZA, NATAL, BRAZIL
PROJECT: 2011–12
REALISATION: 2012–14

The existing structure of the old gymnasium – a concrete field framed by columns and trusses without a roof or walls – defined the starting point. Its geometry is extruded over the entire building area, creating a single large roof. Tweaking the local material palette of cement blocks and corrugated metal roofs to create a lighter space from which the hot air gets blown out, the new gymnasium is a permeable, fully naturally conditioned building with various levels of transparency as well as privacy.

'Mãe Luiza is a place of opposing dynamics: a strong, close-knit community yet heavily affected by crime; a beautiful location beside dunes and the ocean but fenced off by commercial developments. Suffocatingly dense housing plots exist alongside vast open spaces scarcely used at all. In this place of tensions and potential, we collaborated closely with the local community to build this new structure together.'
Ascan Mergenthaler
Senior Partner

MUSÉE UNTERLINDEN
EXTENSION

COLMAR, FRANCE
COMPETITION: 2009
PROJECT: 2010–12
REALISATION: 2012–15

The extension of the historic Unterlinden Museum unites two building complexes that face each other across a square: a medieval convent housing the Isenheim Altarpiece and a new museum building with some former municipal baths. These are connected by an underground gallery reached by a new, cast spiral staircase. The Sinn canal, once hidden, was reopened to become the central element of this new public space. Close to the water, a small building marks the positioning, volume and shape of the mill that once stood there.

'This project encompasses three dimensions: urban development, architecture and museography. We were looking for an urban configuration and architectural language that would fit into the historical context of the medieval city of Colmar and the convent, yet upon closer inspection appear contemporary.'
Christoph Röttinger
Associate Partner

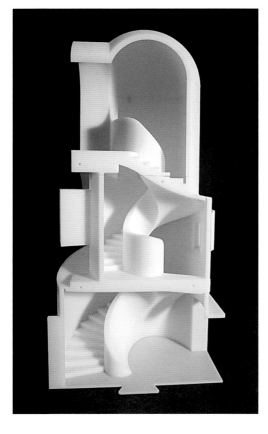

RICOLA KRÄUTERZENTRUM

LAUFEN, SWITZERLAND
PROJECT: 2010–13
REALISATION: 2013–14

Ricola's herb-growing centre has an elongated shape that reflects the stages involved in the industrial processing of herbs, from cutting and drying to blending and storage. Built largely out of rammed earth, the prefabricated elements were manufactured in a nearby factory out of ingredients extracted from local quarries and mines. Loam, marl and material excavated on site were mixed and compacted to create the formwork and then layered in blocks to build the walls.

'The Kräuterzentrum is like a geometrical extrusion of the archaic landscape within which it stands. Inside, the smell of the herbs and presence of earth heighten the experience of nature. Led by principles of ecological balance, the building embodies Ricola's exceptional philosophy and commitment to the environment.'
Stefan Marbach
Senior Partner

CHÄSERRUGG SUMMIT BUILDING

UNTERWASSER, SWITZERLAND
CONCEPT STUDY: 2011
PROJECT: 2013–14
REALISATION: 2014–15

Rising to 2,262 metres, the Chäserrugg is the easternmost of the seven peaks of the Churfirsten mountains. The existing station, a pragmatic steel structure on a concrete foundation typical of the 1970s, remains and has been integrated. The new station and mountain restaurant is constructed in solid wood. A large roof connects the two structures and creates an outdoor arrival hall.

'The new building was prefabricated by local craftspeople in the valley, and assembled on top of the mountain over a summer. The interior was completed the following winter. We decided to use wood because, despite this building's size, we wanted to embed it in the local tradition. Equally important was a thoughtful exploitation of resources: except for the crane, all of the parts required for the building were transported by the cable car in the course of its regular runs.'
Christine Binswanger
Senior Partner

KINDERSPITAL ZÜRICH

ZURICH, SWITZERLAND
COMPETITION: 2011–12
PROJECT: 2014 – PLANNED COMPLETION 2024

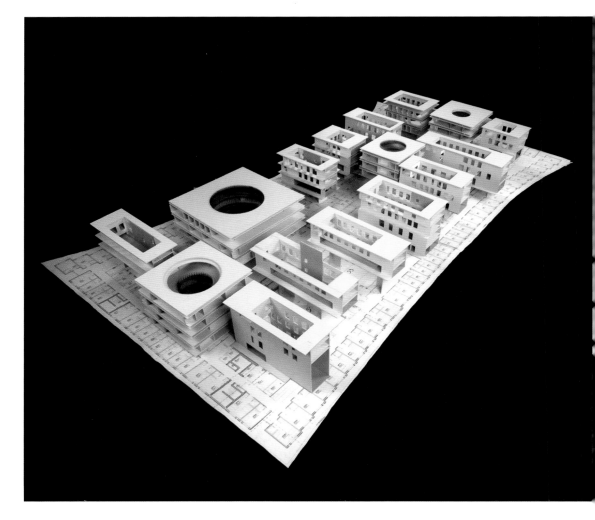

The Kinderspital is the largest hospital in Switzerland for both inpatient and outpatient care of children and adolescents. Its new building has a city-like plan – with streets, intersections and squares – over three floors. Round courtyards give access to the hospital's most important areas, and green inner courtyards provide daylight and allow nature to penetrate deep into the building.

'This building is about an architecture of care, but also about care for architecture: from providing daylight for everyone, to the layout of the many functional units and their interdependencies, to the outdoor play areas for children and how a wood post lands on a small concrete sphere. Everything is meticulously considered and evaluated with all those concerned. The ambience will hopefully not only reduce stress for parents and children, but provide a hospital where staff will enjoy working.'
Christine Binswanger
Senior Partner

'We thought about how to improve life when experienced from a hospital bed. A patient, especially a young one, doesn't always just want rest, but also needs freedom of movement and encounters with others. Besides the nice rooms they stay in, there are many different and pleasant gathering places, and kids and parents can easily find their way around.'
Jacques Herzog
Founder

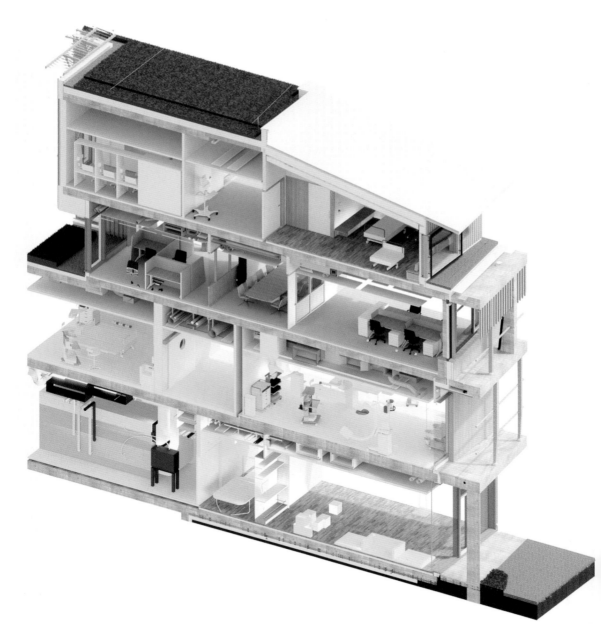

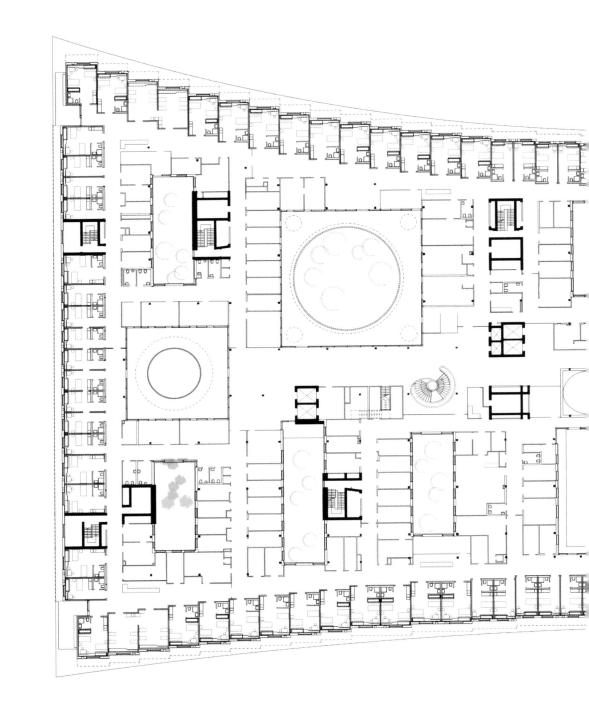

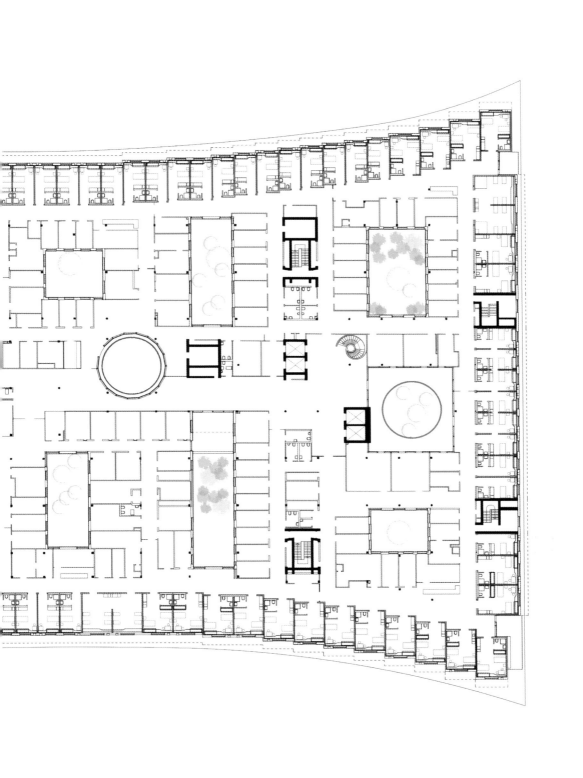

STADTCASINO BASEL
EXTENSION

BASEL, SWITZERLAND
PROJECT: 2012–16
REALISATION: 2016–20

Built in 1876, Basel's concert hall – the Musiksaal – is one of the oldest and most important in Europe. Its extension to accommodate contemporary needs was achieved by encasing the existing building within new and precise simulacra of its original elevations to provide spacious foyers, backstage facilities for performers, and technical services. Loggia-like recesses were added to the expansive staircases, giving people additional space during intervals.

'Outside, we simulated the historic façade using wood instead of the masonry and plaster of the time. Inside, nineteenth-century stylistic elements such as velvet and mirror are revitalised by the artificial forms and colours of the materials. The new extension grows out of the old building as if it had always been there.'
Andreas Fries
Partner

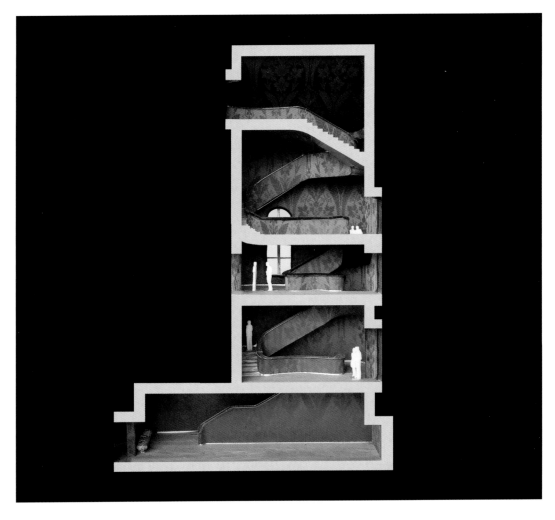

M+

HONG KONG
COMPETITION: 2012–13
PROJECT AND REALISATION: 2013–21

M+ is a cultural centre for twentieth- and twenty-first-century art, design, architecture and the moving image. Above an inviting public plaza, a horizontal slab of exhibition spaces is surmounted by a vertical extension housing studio, curatorial and research spaces. Sun-shading horizontal louvres with an integrated LED lighting system transform the vertical façade into an immense display screen for works of art.

'Initially an obstacle, the underground railway tunnels beneath the site have become the distinctive feature of M+. The uncovering of these "found" spaces has resulted in a space of unprecedented potential for art and design, installation and performance – a stage for unique experiences, inseparable from the specific character of the location.'
Ascan Mergenthaler
Senior Partner

'M+ is a public destination – open from all sides, there are many ways of accessing and moving through the building. People can take shelter under the podium right next to the park, sit on the generous public topography of the Grand Stair in the atrium, or climb up to the rooftop garden to meet and enjoy panoramic views of the harbour. The display screen is another way the M+ building engages not only visitors but the city of Hong Kong at large by bringing art into the public domain.'
Wim Walschap
Partner

NATIONAL LIBRARY OF ISRAEL

JERUSALEM, ISRAEL
COMPETITION: 2013
PROJECT: 2013 – PLANNED COMPLETION 2023

A rethinking of the library both as an institution and a building type, the National Library of Israel is open and transparent but grounded in the traditions of the great world libraries and of Jerusalem itself. Seen from the Knesset (Parliament), the curved shape of the library preserves views of the western landscape. Carved stone binds the building together; the elevated form provides shade while its mineral construction adds thermal mass to insulate the interior spaces.

'What is the role of a library? Since its inception, the design of the National Library has been guided by the central value of democratising knowledge, to bring the institution's collections and resources to as broad and diverse an audience as possible. The building will bring people together to study, to do their work individually, while also becoming a place for people to simply be with and around others.'
Jason Frantzen
Senior Partner

MKM MUSEUM KÜPPERSMÜHLE
EXTENSION

DUISBURG, GERMANY
PROJECT: 2013–17
REALISATION: 2016–21

This former mill with its historic brick elevations houses an art museum containing one of the finest collections of German works from the 1950s to the present. Adjoining the vast grey silos, the extension's dimensions and materials accord with the existing brick structures. The new architecture and interior design are based on the overall character of the Küppersmühle as a typical industrial facility of the nineteenth and twentieth centuries.

'The extension fits into the chain of impressive historical brick structures and rounds off the existing museum complex. Completing the entire row of buildings within the harbour basin, the project represents a complementary integration of urban planning and architecture.'
Robert Hösl
Partner

Making Windows in Sandcastles
Ricky Burdett (pages 14–37)
1   Interview with the author, August 2022.
2   Rowan Moore, 'Herzog & de Meuron: 'Architecture Is the
    Art of Facts. We Shouldn't Have a Moralistic Standpoint',
    The Guardian, 31 October 2021, https://www.theguardian.
    com/artanddesign/2021/oct/31/herzog-and-de-meuron-
    m-plus-astrazeneca-national-library-of-israel-stadtcasino-
    one-park-drive-royal-college-of-art.
3   As co-editor of the *9H* architecture magazine and
    director of the 9H Gallery in London, the author published
    and exhibited some of these early works between 1983
    and 1989. He was also a member of the jury for the
    Tate Modern competition in 1994/95.
4   Roger Diener, Jacques Herzog, Marcel Meili, Pierre de
    Meuron and Christian Schmid, *Switzerland: An Urban
    Portrait*, ETH Studio Basel, Contemporary City Institute,
    vols 1–4, Basel, 2006.
5   'Jacques Herzog: Letter to David Chipperfield', *Domus*,
    October 2020, https://www.domusweb.it/en/architecture/
    2020/10/13/jacques-herzog-letter-from-basel.html.

Spaces of Potential
Vicky Richardson (pages 50–59)
1   'Jacques Herzog: Letter to David Chipperfield', *Domus*,
    October 2020, https://www.domusweb.it/en/architecture/
    2020/10/13/jacques-herzog-letter-from-basel.html.
2   See Gerhard Mack, *Herzog & de Meuron 1992–1996:
    The Complete Works*, vol. 3, Basel, 2000, pp. 13–19.
3   Herzog & de Meuron, 'Urban Suburban', in Dan Graham,
    The Suburban City, exh. cat., Kunstmuseum Basel, 1996,
    pp. 25–8 (in German), 43–5 (in English).
4   Lord Rogers of Riverside, *Towards an Urban Renaissance*,
    London, 1999.
5   See Gerhard Mack, *Herzog & de Meuron 2002–2004:
    The Complete Works*, vol. 5, Basel, 2020, p. 125.
6   See Gerhard Mack, *Herzog & de Meuron 1997–2001:
    The Complete Works*, vol. 4, Basel, 2009, p. 41.
7   Public London Charter, 8 October 2021.

Different Takes
Herzog & de Meuron: Architecture and Perception
Beate Söntgen (pages 60–65)
1   *Anpassung und Setzung*, VHS, PAL, colour, 55 min.
2   These two stills are reproduced in Philip Ursprung,
    'Exhibiting Herzog & de Meuron', in Philip Ursprung (ed.),
    Herzog & de Meuron: Natural History, exh. cat., Canadian
    Centre for Architecture, Montreal, 2002–03, p. 14.
3   Michel de Certeau, 'Gehen in der Stadt', in Michel de Certeau,
    Kunst des Handelns [1980], trans. Ronald Voullié, Berlin,
    1988, pp. 179–208.
4   Robin Evans, 'Figures, Doors and Passages' [1978], in
    Robin Evans, *Translations from Drawing to Building and
    Other Essays*, London, 1997, pp. 55–91.
5   Timothy Ingold, 'Building, Dwelling, Living', in Marilyn
    Strathern, *Shifting Contexts*, London and New York, 1995,
    pp. 57–80.
6   Timothy Ingold, 'Epilogue: Towards a Politics of Dwelling',
    Conservation & Society, vol. 3, no. 2 (July–December 2005),
    pp. 501–08, p. 503.
7   https://www.youtube.com/watch?v=rM1-zHCLG9g.

Building for More than Healthcare
Henrik Schødts (pages 70–77)
1   From the Benny Andersen poem *Langt Lavere Marker*, 1974.
    Author's translation.

SELECTED BIBLIOGRAPHY

General

Herzog & de Meuron. Architektur Denkform,
Architekturmuseum Basel, 1988

Herzog & de Meuron, El Croquis, 60 (1983–93), 84
(1993–97), 109/110 (1998–2002), 129/139 (2002–06),
152/153 (2005–10), Madrid, 1993/1997/2002/2006/2010

Thomas Ruff, Architectures of Herzog & de Meuron:
Portraits by Thomas Ruff, New York, 1994

Herzog & de Meuron, a+u, 300, Special Issue 2/2002
(1978–2002), Special Issue 8/2006 (2002–06), Tokyo,
1995/2002/2006

Gerhard Mack, Herzog & de Meuron: The Complete Works,
6 vols: vol. 1, 1978–88; vol. 2, 1989–91; vol. 3, 1992–96;
vol. 4, 1997–2001, vol. 5, 2002–04, vol. 6, 2005–07,
Basel, 1997/1996/2000/2009/2020/2018

Herzog & de Meuron. Zeichnungen. Drawings, New York, 1997

Philip Ursprung (ed.), Herzog & de Meuron: Natural History,
exh. cat., Canadian Centre for Architecture, Montreal,
2002–03

Cristina Bechtler (ed.), Pictures of Architecture – Architecture
of Pictures: A Conversation between Jacques Herzog and
Jeff Wall moderated by Philip Ursprung, Vienna/New York,
2004

Theodora Vischer (ed.), Vademecum. Herzog & de Meuron.
No. 250. An Exhibition, Basel, 2004

Jean-François Chevrier, From Basel – Herzog & de Meuron,
Basel, 2016

Herzog & de Meuron, AV Monografías: Herzog & de Meuron
1978–2002 (vol. 1), Herzog & de Meuron 2003–19 (vol. 2),
Madrid, 2019

Dino Simonett (ed.), Herzog & de Meuron 001–500. Index
of the Work of Herzog & de Meuron 1978–2019. A Tribute and
a Celebration, Basel, 2019

'Jacques Herzog: Letter to David Chipperfield', Domus,
October 2020, https://www.domusweb.it/en/architecture/
2020/10/13/jacques-herzog-letter-from-basel.html

ETH Studio, Basel

Roger Diener, Jacques Herzog, Marcel Meili, Pierre de
Meuron and Christian Schmid, Switzerland: An Urban Portrait,
ETH Studio Basel, Contemporary City Institute, vols 1–4,
Basel, 2006

Roger Diener, Jacques Herzog, Marcel Meili, Pierre de
Meuron, Manuel Herz, Christian Schmid and Milica Topalovic,
The Inevitable Specificity of Cities, ETH Studio Basel,
Contemporary City Institute, Zurich, 2015

Individual projects

Rowan Moore and Raymund Ryan (eds), Herzog & de Meuron:
Building Tate Modern, London, 2000

Herzog & de Meuron, Prada Aoyama Tokyo: Herzog & de
Meuron, Germano Celant (ed.), second edition, Milan, 2003

Sophie O'Brien (ed.), Herzog & de Meuron + Ai Weiwei:
Serpentine Gallery Pavilion 2012, London, 2012

Gerhard Mack (ed.), Herzog & de Meuron: Transforming Park
Avenue Armory New York, Basel, 2014

Gerhard Mack, Sieben Bauten. Seven Buildings 1983–2014.
Ricola – Herzog & de Meuron, Laufen, 2014

Chris Dercon and Nicholas Serota (eds), Tate Modern:
Building a Museum for the 21st Century, London, 2016

Jacques Herzog and Pierre de Meuron, Treacherous
Transparencies: Thoughts and Observations Triggered by
a Visit to the Farnsworth House, Barcelona, 2016

Nobuyuki Yoshida and Herzog & de Meuron (eds), Herzog &
de Meuron: Elbphilharmonie, a+u, Tokyo, 558, March 2017

Gerhard Mack and Herzog & de Meuron (eds), Herzog &
de Meuron: Elbphilharmonie Hamburg, Basel, 2018

Nicholas Olsberg (ed.), The Kramlich Residence and Collection,
Berlin, 2019

Ion de Andrade, Tomislav Dushanov, Nicole Miescher and
Lars Müller (eds), Mãe Luíza: Building Optimism, with the
story 'Creating a New Sun' by Paulo Lins, Zurich, 2021

PHOTOGRAPHIC ACKNOWLEDGEMENTS

Every attempt has been made to trace the copyright holders of works reproduced. Specific acknowledgements are as follows:

Photo © Iñigo Aguirre: fig. 12. Photo © Albatross: pp. 146–47. Photo © Architekturzentrum Wien, Collection, photo: Margherita Spiluttini: pp. 8, 80–83, 85, 88–89, 148; figs 9, 10, 15, 17, 37. Photo © Arup: p. 140. Photo © Iwan Baan: pp. 2–5, 12–13, 100–01, 103 (bottom), 105, 107–09, 111 (bottom), 114 (right © Vitra), 115, 117, 118 (bottom), 119–21, 125, 142–43; figs 41–43. Photo © David Barreiro: p. 91; figs 35, 36, 39, 40. Photo © ADRIANO A. BIONDO / BIONDOPICTURES: fig. 20. © 2023 Calder Foundation, New York / DACS, London: fig. 30. Photo © Katalin Deér: pp 127–29; figs 16, 18, 19. Photo © Gina Folly: p. 158; figs 8, 21. Film stills © Ulrich Gambke, Courtesy of Nauman Film GmbH, Munich, 1995: fig. 44. Photo © Jonathan Grevsen: fig. 53. © Andreas Gursky / Courtesy Sprüth Magers Berlin London / DACS 2023: fig. 34. © Herzog & de Meuron: pp. 84, 86, 90, 92, 98, 99, 102, 103 (top), 104, 106, 110, 111 (top), 114 (left), 116, 118 (top), 122 (left), 124, 126, 130–36, 141 (top), 144, 145; figs 3, 4, 6, 22–24, 26, 27, 29, 30, 49–52. Photo © Jacques Herzog und Pierre de Meuron Kabinett, Basel, photo: Serge Hasenböhler: fig. 2. Photo © Robert Hösl: figs 1, 32, 33. Photo © Hufton + Crow: fig. 38. Photo © Hufton + Crow and MBEACH1, LLLP: pp. 112–13. Photo © Kevin Mak: p. 141 (bottom); fig. 13. Photo © Duccio Malagamba, Barcelona: fig. 11. Photo © Simon Menges: pp. 6, 149–51; fig. 48. Photo © Nacása & Partners: p. 96; fig. 28. Photo © Erika Overmeer and MBEACH1, LLLP: fig. 14. Photo © Christian Richters / VIEW: p. 97. © Thomas Ruff, DACS 2023: figs 46, 47. Photo © Shinkenchiku-sha: p. 87. Photo © Ruedi Walti: pp. 1, 10, 93–95, 122 (right), 123, 137; figs 7, 31, 45. Photo © Roman Weyeneth: pp 138–39; fig. 5.

INDEX

Page numbers in *italics* refer to illustrations

Herzog & de Meuron is an international architectural practice based in Basel, Switzerland. Established in 1978, the practice is led by the two founders together with the Partners and the CEO. Today, an international team of over 600 collaborators is engaged in a wide range of projects across Europe, the Americas and Asia. The main office in Basel works in tandem with studios in Berlin and Munich, Paris, London, Hong Kong, New York and San Francisco, and our site offices in Copenhagen, Jerusalem and Hangzhou. Awards received include the Pritzker Architecture Prize (USA) in 2001, the RIBA Gold Medal (UK), the Praemium Imperiale (Japan), both in 2007, and the Mies Crown Hall Americas Prize (USA) in 2014.

Founding Partners
Jacques Herzog
Pierre de Meuron

Senior Partners
Christine Binswanger
Jason Frantzen
Stefan Marbach
Ascan Mergenthaler
Esther Zumsteg

Partners
Simon Demeuse
Santiago Espitia Berndt
Andreas Fries
Robert Hösl
Martin Knüsel
Wim Walschap

Associate Partners
Olga Bolshanina
Steffen Riegas
Christoph Röttinger
Tobias Winkelmann

CEO
Adrian Keller

Associates
Mark Bähr
Michael Bär
Maximilian Beckenbauer
Michael Bekker
Jack Brough
Aurélien Caetano
Delphine Camus
Edman Choy
Thomas de Vries
Arnaud Delugeard
Linxi Dong
Michael Drobnik
Tomislav Dushanov
Silja Ebert
Andrea Erpenbeck
Birgit Föllmer
Alexander Franz
Michel Frei
Martin Fröhlich
Stefan Goeddertz
Sebastian Hefti
Adriana Hernández Arteaga
Paul Kath
Thorsten Kemper
Yasmin Kherad
Martin Krapp
Nicholas Lyons
Donald Mak
Dieter Mangold
Alfonso Miguel Caballero
Kwamina Monney
Helen Ng
Mehmet Noyan
Alexa Nürnberger
John O'Mara
Julian Oggier
Enrique Peláez
Alexander Reichert
Andrea Rüegsegger
Philip Schmerbeck
Marc Schmidt
Michael Schmidt
Iva Smrke
Lukasz Szlachcic
Milou Teeling
Ilia Stefanov Tsachev
Stephan Weber
Tristan Zelic

First published on the occasion of the exhibition
Herzog & de Meuron

Royal Academy of Arts
14 July – 15 October 2023

Supported by Stefan Bollinger with additional support
from Laura and Scott Malkin and   swiss arts council

pr:helvetia

Herzog & de Meuron
Jacques Herzog
Pierre de Meuron
Christine Binswanger
Esther Zumsteg
Donald Mak
Mathieu Bujnowskyj
Saakib Sait
with
Roman Aebi
Giorgio Azzariti
Martin Cassani
Ainsley Johnston
Sarah Kim
Stefanie Manthey
Nikola Miloradovic
Günter Schwob
Milou Teeling
Victor Tessler
Edward Wang

Royal Academy of Arts
Giulia Ariete, Rights and Repro Manager
Rebecca Bailey, Exhibition Manager
Guy Carr, Assistant Exhibition Manager
Vicky Richardson, Head of Architecture and
    Drue Heinz Curator
Andrea Tarsia, Director of Exhibitions
Rose Thompson, Assistant Curator

Royal Academy Publications
Florence Dassonville, Production and
    Distribution Co-ordinator
Carola Krueger, Production and Distribution Manager
Peter Sawbridge, Head of Publishing and
    Editorial Director

Translation from the German (Beate Söntgen):
    Fiona Elliott
Copy-editing and proofreading: Caroline Ellerby
Design: Martin Perrin/Perrin Studio
Colour origination: DawkinsColour, London

Printed in Italy by Printer Trento Srl

British Library Cataloguing-in-Publication Data
A catalogue record for this book is available from the
British Library

ISBN 978-1-912520-71-8

Distributed outside the United States and Canada by
ACC Art Books Ltd, Riverside House, Dock Lane, Melton,
Woodbridge, IP12 1PE

Distributed in the United States and Canada by
ARTBOOK | D.A.P., 75 Broad Street, Suite 630,
New York, NY 10004

Illustrations
Page 1: View of Basel showing the towers of the
    Roche pharmaceutical complex in the distance
Pages 2–3: Aerial view of the harbourside in Hamburg,
    showing the Elbphilharmonie
Pages 4–5: Tate Modern, London
Page 6: MKM Museum Küppersmühle, Duisburg
Page 8: REHAB Basel
Page 10: Stadtcasino Basel
Pages 12–13: Interior of Herzog & de Meuron's *Kabinett*
    at their Helsinki Dreispitz building, Basel
Page 158: Workspace at Herzog & de Meuron's
    Rheinschanze 6 campus